W9-DGS-299

The Great American Candy Bar Book

The Great American Candy Bar Book

Ray Broekel

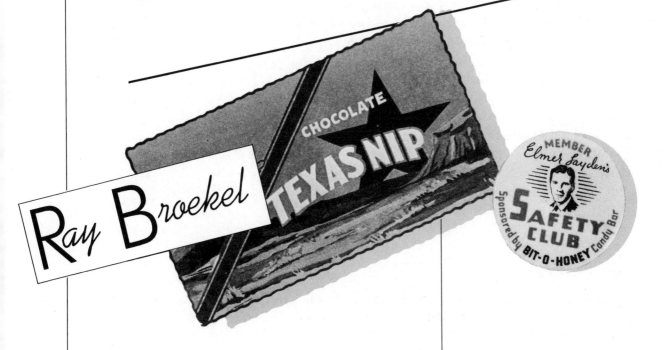

Houghton Mifflin Company   Boston   1982

To the memory of Eugene and Hedwig Broekel,
German immigrants, who believed in the American Dream
and made it come true.

Author's Note

I'd appreciate hearing from anyone who has uncovered a
batch of old candy bar wrappers in a musty attic or in a
dark, damp basement. I'd also appreciate hearing from
those of you with fond memories of candy bars you can
share. Perhaps there are enough of us around to form the
Great American Candy Bar Club.

Ray Broekel
c/o Houghton Mifflin Company
2 Park Street
Boston, Massachusetts 02108

Copyright © 1982 by Ray Broekel

All rights reserved. No part of this work may be reproduced or
transmitted in any form or by any means, electronic or mechan-
ical, including photocopying and recording, or by any information storage or retrieval system, except as may be expressly per-
mitted by the 1976 Copyright Act or in writing from the
publisher. Requests for permission should be addressed in writing
to Houghton Mifflin Company, 2 Park Street, Boston, Massachusetts 02108.

Library of Congress Cataloging in Publication Data
Broekel, Ray.
  The great American candy bar book.

  1. Candy industry — United States — History. I. Title.
HD9330.C653U525 1982   338.7′664153′0973   82-6248
ISBN 0-395-32502-1 (pbk.)   AACR2

Printed in the United States of America

M 10 9 8 7 6 5 4 3 2 1

Book design by Edith Allard, Designworks

The National Candy Buyers Bar Survey on pages 153–56 is
reprinted courtesy of *Candy & Snack Industry/Candy Marketer.*

Acknowledgments

Special thanks to all those companies in the candy industry that cooperated by providing me with materials for this book.

Special thanks are also extended individually to Hank Bornhofft, Nate Sloane, Joe Blumenthal, Ben Myerson, Robert Welch, Ruth Patterson, Helene Kline Mooty, Bob Fortunato, Eileen Gordon, Kim Payne, Susan A. Graham, Michael S. Gotkin, Joan T. Buckley, Richard S. Gates, Domenic M. Antonellis, Rose St. John, Betty Garrett, Eric Alexander, Franklin Wyman, Jr., Ted Hauff, David Stivers, Jack Sevick, Jr., Hollis Gerrish, Greg Spangler, and Glenn Sontag.

Individual thanks also to James E. Mack, Helen LaPat Smith, Mike Lench, Rita V. Fogler, Sherry Foote, Eleanor Cristofano, R. Melvin Goetze, Edgar R. Goldenberg, Vincent P. Donohue, Court Sanders, Marty Grotz, John H. Bleke, Jimmy Miller, Nancy Tobias-Kendzie, Russ Larson, John A. Buzzard, Penny Buzzard, Joseph K. DeLapp, Ned Bjornson, Leslie A. Kogan, David Foy, Nello V. Ferrara, John Trainor, B. E. Atkinson, Jerry Claeys, Jr., Ron Salek, Robert J. Harrington, Nancy Coward, Robert L. Mack, Edward Ansel, Deborah DeDomenico, Catherine Blankenship, Homer Rothleitner, Robert J. Harmsen, John Flood, Oscar Boldemann, Jr., Robert D. Lewis, Jackie Darling, Lawrence F. Dalicandro, Polly Bressack, Erich Fritsch, Ned E. Mitchell, Kathy Kelly, Robin Hill, Ralph Lewis, Karen Cverko, and Al Swetich.

My apologies to those candy bars that have been overlooked in this presentation. Editorial judgment has been used in establishing dates and other data where discrepancies occurred in reference sources. Last of all, thanks to my editors, Tom Hart and Laura Nash, and copy editor, Frances Apt. They really helped make the manuscript readable.

Contents

Preface

Pleasant memories of how good candy bars tasted when I was a kid in the 1930s led to the writing of this book. While doing my research, I found that today's candy bars taste pretty good, too. So let out another notch in the belt, Sam.

Introduction

The candy bar is as American as the hamburger, the hot dog, doughnuts, potato chips, and the ice cream cone, and ranks as the favorite food of millions of people from one to one hundred. Our love affair with the candy bar began back in 1894, when Milton S. Hershey manufactured the first American chocolate bars, the Hershey Almond Bar and the Hershey Milk Chocolate Bar.

Bunte Brothers was the firm credited as the first to make a chocolate-coated bar. And according to the National Confectioners Association, in 1911 baseball fans ate the first combination candy bars, individually wrapped and made up of such combined ingredients as almond nougats and chocolate-coated marshmallows with peanuts. Another report, however, says the Goo Goo Cluster was the first of the combination bars; it was produced in 1912. Credit for the first candy bar to be manufactured west of the Mississippi River goes to the Cherry Mash candy bar. Perley G. Gerrish had the distinction of originating the peanut bar in 1905 — the Squirrel Brand Peanut Bar.

At first, candy bars were generally in the dime category, but sales weren't too terrific, because a customer could go into any dime store and buy a pound of loose candy for just ten cents — a much better buy than a candy bar weighing four ounces. Right after World War I, when there was a drop in sugar and chocolate prices, bars often sold for five cents apiece. (In the Depression, five-cent candy bars, and one-cent versions of some of the brands, became the norm.)

Milton S. Hershey and other chocolate manufacturers shipped large slabs of solid chocolate to army training camps around the country. At the camps the slabs were cut into smaller blocks, weighed, and the blocks distributed to the doughboys. That task became too time-consuming at the bases, so the manufacturers began wrapping chocolate bars individually for shipment to army camps.

After the war, confectioners realized that the wrapped candy bar was a good commercial product, and bars began popping up here and there. Some of the trade names used then are still around today, though the manufacturer's name has probably changed (several times, in some cases). Several of the manufacturers were located in Illinois then, mainly in the Chicago area. Being in the Midwest put them in close proximity to many of the raw materials they needed.

During World War II the candy bar allowed G.I. Joe to form friendships with those whose language he couldn't speak. But it was more than an ambassador of good will; it became a universal medium of exchange.

Pretty much kept at the five-cent level into the 1960s, the candy bar moved back up to ten cents in 1968 because of rising costs. In the 1970s, fifteen cents, twenty-five cents, and thirty cents became the going prices. And in the 1980s, bars costing thirty-five cents and up appeared on the market.

The Makings: Basics

Chocolate is a product of the cacao tree, found in Central and South America and West Africa. Seeds (beans) are scooped out of the tree's pods at harvest time, put through a fermentation process, are sun-dried, and then bagged for shipment.

At a chocolate factory the beans are cleaned and roasted, and then are cracked and broken into hard bits called nibs. After various grades and flavors of nibs are blended, they are ground up. The grinding process turns the nibs into what's called chocolate liquor, and this liquor is subjected to pressure until cocoa butter — a vegetable fat in the chocolate — is released. The cocoa butter is put aside for the time being, and the remaining liquor is allowed to set at room temperature. Bars made from this hardened plain liquor are unsweetened chocolate. However, if sugar and the correct amount of cocoa butter are added before the liquor hardens, the result is sweet chocolate. When milk solids are added to the sweet chocolate formula, the end product is milk chocolate. These, then, are the basic stuffs used in candy bars, among other products.

How did the nougat center come about? Back in the eighteenth century, so the story goes, a kindly old lady who lived in the French village of Montelimer made her own sweet concoction of honey, sugar, nuts, fruits, and eggs to pass out among her friends and relatives. The friends and relatives, appreciative of being on the receiving end of the culinary treats, responded by saying, "*Tu nous gâtes*" (You spoil us). From the old lady's recipe we get the filling; from the expression of thanks, we get the word *nougat*.

Here's one version of how fudge was created. Caramels were being produced in a Philadelphia confectionery when the head cook suddenly realized that someone had goofed. Instead of a chewy caramel, what had emerged was a finely crystallized nonchewy substance. In disgust the head cook uttered, "Fudge! Bah!" and so, because of the goof, fudge was born. And if you're a fudge lover, hooray for goofs.

Caramel, so one story goes, is credited to a Chicago confectioner of many years ago. The confectioner decided to add cream or milk solids to a butterscotch he was producing. These solids were intended to improve the flavor and texture, but as the confectioner kept adding the milk element, he suddenly realized that he had completely changed the character of the butterscotch. What he had done was to create a new confection, caramel!

Marshmallows were familiar to the ancient Egyptians, who considered a real delicacy the root of the mallow tree, dried and pulverized. Today the following ingredients are common to marshmallows: sugar, corn syrup, gelatin, water, and flavoring.

Chocolate, nougat, fudge, caramel, marshmallow — these, along with coconut and various other nuts, are the main ingredients in most candy bars, although there are some others, as we'll see.

Confectionery firms today are located all over the country, and most of them operate almost entirely on an automated basis. The automated production process is not complete until each piece or stick of candy or bar has been wrapped, packaged, boxed, or bagged. According to the National Confectioners Association, it takes just about a minute to wrap around 110 candy bars by machine, seal 180 bags of orange-flavored slices, wrap 600 pieces of hard candy, or wrap 750 pieces of toffee or caramel. In the early days candy was individually wrapped, but no company could exist today without automation. As one plant foreman put it, "People today just wouldn't work under the conditions that were around in the early years."

Candy bars that are chocolate-covered (about 70 percent of them are) go through a machine called an enrober. The candy centers, arranged on a moving belt, pass over a little pool of chocolate, which coats the undersides of the bars. The undercoated bars move under a curtain of chocolate that deposits just the right amount of chocolate on the top. Now completely enrobed, the bars go through a cooling tunnel at a rate of about 700 bars a minute before being delivered to automatic wrapping machines. After they've been wrapped, the bars are boxed either by machine or by hand, usually twenty-four or thirty-six to a box. The boxes are then packed into larger shipping containers.

It is in these containers that each bar starts the long trip that ends with it in the hand of someone looking for a treat. And, as the following pages should show, there is no more delicious treat than the great American candy bar and some of the other products closely related to it.

If at First You Don't Succeed, Try Again and Again and Again

Milton S. Hershey opened his own candy business after learning about the candy trade while working for Joseph H. Royer, a confectioner in Lancaster, Pennsylvania. Milton set up his place in Philadelphia in 1876, but the business didn't pan out and was sold six years later.

Hershey went on to Chicago, then to New York, setting up candy businesses in both cities, failing in both cities. Then it was back to Pennsylvania Dutch country, where Milton had been raised. Before long, he was making caramels, the fresh-milk way, in Lancaster. One kind, named McGinties, was bean-shaped and was sold to kids ten for a penny. Some of his other caramel products were Jim Cracks, Lotuses, Coconut Ices, Uniques, and Empires, and so was born the Lancaster Caramel Company. Hershey achieved much of his early success by selling his products in England. But even though he was doing well with his caramels, he didn't feel he had made a real success of himself in the candy business.

In 1893, he visited the World's Columbian Exposition in Chicago, where he saw a marvelous display of chocolate-making machinery brought over from Germany. Knowing that the chocolate market was growing rapidly in the United States, he decided to install some of the chocolate-making machines in his Lancaster factory. Before long, he was turning out chocolate to coat his caramels and to make such novelties as chocolate cigars and cigarettes and blossom-shaped chocolate pieces called Chrysanthemums and Sweet Peas. The Hershey Almond Bar and Hershey Milk Chocolate Bar first appeared in 1894.

Convinced that the chocolate business was the one he wanted to be in, Hershey sold the Lancaster Caramel Company plant for $1 million in 1900 to the American Caramel Company of New York. (A Lancaster Caramel Company plant located in Bloomington, Illinois, was sold separately to the Paul F. Beich Company.) Hershey retained all rights to his chocolate-making machinery, however.

After a trip to Europe with his wife in 1900, Hershey bought some farmland in Derry Church, Pennsylvania, his birthplace, and built a new factory right in the middle of the cornfields. A town, which he planned, grew up around it, and the factory went into operation in 1904.

As the town grew, it became evident that a post office was needed, so a contest with a prize of $100 was held to find "the best suitable name." Hersheykoko won the prize, but fortunately it was soon shortened to Hershey.

One of the more popular items, Hershey Kisses, was introduced in 1907. The kisses were wrapped, but the identification plumes weren't added until 1921. In the late 1920s came Eatmors, which were unwrapped ribbed kisses packaged in a tube.

Hershey's business prospered. During World War II, the firm produced for the government a specially formulated chocolate bar that wouldn't melt in a soldier's pocket, but would sustain that soldier if no other food was available. Called Field Ration D, the bar was made of a combination of ingredients, but chocolate was the main one. About 500,000 bars were turned out each hour, twenty-four hours a day, at the Hershey factory. Each four-ounce bar provided 600 calories. Although not the best-tasting candy bar (a fact to which I can personally attest), the bar did serve the purpose of providing a quick-energy pickup.

The Hershey Almond Bar and Hershey Milk Chocolate Bar sold for five cents until November 11, 1969. From then on, increased raw material and overhead costs necessitated a change in the selling price. The Hershey people, like most other manufacturers, tried to counter rising costs by gradually upping the selling price, and bar weights were raised or lowered in response to fluctuating costs.

The Hershey Company experienced healthy growth at the close of World War II, and today stands as one of the foremost manufacturers of chocolate products in the world.

Gimme a Good Bite, Buddy

Mr. Goodbar, a big success for the Hershey Company, appeared on the candy bar scene in 1925. It was made of a chocolate with a different consistency from the smooth milk chocolate in other Hershey bars. And embedded in the chocolate were peanuts. The bar was thin but long and wide, so kids with limited funds found it a good buy. Also, kids who liked the combination of peanuts and chocolate bought Mr. Goodbar rather than the Hershey Milk Chocolate Bar or the Hershey Almond Bar. The different-textured chocolate, however, didn't appeal to lovers of smoother chocolate. Over the years Mr. Goodbar has decreased in size but still has its share of the peanut-cum-chocolate lovers' market. It's been around for over fifty years and is still going strong.

During the 1930s, very small versions of Mr. Goodbar, Hershey Milk Chocolate, and Hershey Honey-Almond Milk Chocolate bars were available for a penny apiece from vending machines. (Such a vending machine, fully operational, is sitting in my living room, filled with small candy bars. When you put a penny in the slot, a candy bar comes out. The difference between now and 1930 is that what costs one cent now to come out, costs about nine cents to put in.)

Several basic foods are used in the manufacture of Mr. Goodbar and other Hershey products, among them, cocoa

beans, milk, sugar, almonds, and peanuts. The storage facility at Hershey can hold about ninety million pounds of cocoa beans. That's enough for about five and a half billion Hershey bars.

Fresh whole milk, purchased from more than a thousand farms in the vicinity of Hershey plants, is kept in the Hershey storage silos, which have a capacity of more than 150,000 gallons. Enough milk to supply all the people in a city approximately the size of Philadelphia is used each day by Hershey.

Most of the sugar used in the East is cane sugar, imported through Eastern ports. The Hershey's Western plant, located in Oakdale, California, uses both beet sugar and cane sugar, processed in California.

All the almonds used by Hershey are grown in California. The candy maker is the largest single user of almonds in America.

My Cup Floweth Over

H. B. Reese was an employee of Milton S. Hershey's for a number of years. In 1923, Reese opened his own factory, also located in the town of Hershey, and began manufacturing Reese's Peanut Butter Cups. They quickly became famous, because both kids and adults had

a hard time keeping their fingers off that winning combination of milk chocolate and peanut butter.

The Reese family sold the business to Hershey forty years later. Reese's Peanut Butter Cups are now one of the most popular items in the Hershey line. Reese's Crunchy Peanut Butter Cups were introduced in 1976; Reese's Peanut Butter Flavored Chips in 1977. In 1978 Reese's Pieces were introduced. This is the candy used to make the trail that the lovable space creature followed in the movie *E.T.*

Another company, Y&S Candies, Inc., which makes licorice products, was acquired by Hershey in 1977. Some well-known Y&S products are Y&S Twizzlers, first manufactured in 1928, and Nibs, which came along in 1923. Other Y&S products still on the market are Twizzler Bites, Twizzler Strings, All Kinds, and Bassett's Allsorts.

Crispy, and Chocolatey, Too

In 1938, the Hershey Company came out with Krackel, a bar that combined crisped rice with milk chocolate. Krackel quickly caught on with the eating and buying public.

Over the years the Hershey Company experimented with many kinds of bars. Some that fell by the wayside were Honey Almond Nougat (1930s–1942), Mild and Mellow Bar (1933–1941), Aero Bar (1935–1939), Biscrisp Bar (1938–1939), Semi-Sweet Bar (1949–1971), Rally Bar (1970–1978), and Toffo (1975–1978). Two early bars, dates unknown, were the Homestead Bar and the Cloverdale Bar.

Some products of Hershey that still survive are Tropical Chocolate Bar, introduced in 1943; Butter Chip Bar, 1963; Kit Kat, imported from Europe in 1970 and first produced in Hershey in 1973. Rolo came from Europe in 1971 and was first produced in the United States in 1978. After Eight, 1972; Golden Almond, 1977; Whatchamacallit, in 1978. There's also a Special Dark bar, and the new Skor, a chocolate-coated toffee bar.

Milton S. Hershey refused to advertise until 1970, saying, "Give them quality. That's the best kind of advertising." Now the company advertises in newspapers and magazines, on radio and TV in order to maintain its share of the consumer market.

The Hershey Foods Corporation, of which the Hershey Chocolate Company is a division, is conscientious about the promotion it directs to children and is also an industry leader in providing nutritional information on wrappers and labels. It's been doing so on a voluntary basis since 1974.

The Hershey management, like that of almost all candy manufacturers, allows employees to eat as much candy as they wish while on the job, but samples can't be taken home. So for all you unemployed candy lovers out there, here's a job with a real plus!

Where Do They Go Ga Ga over the Goo Goo?

Who concocted the world's first combination candy bar, and when? Standard Candy Company of Nashville, Tennessee, claims the record. In a copper kettle, in 1912, there was placed a mixture of caramel, marshmallow, fresh roasted peanuts, and milk chocolate. The cooked and packaged result was the first Goo Goo Cluster bar. Many versions of how the name Goo Goo was chosen come down to us today, all deriving from the notion of "goo-goo" as a common first utterance.

Because of production-capability limitations, Goo Goo sales have been limited to a few Southern states. But Goo Goo Cluster fans scattered throughout the country can get the bars through direct mail service. Fan orders have come in from California, Massachusetts, Texas, Florida, Montana, and Canada, to name just a few homes of Goo Goo Cluster eaters.

Goo Goo Clusters even had a role in a movie. Since they are something of an institution in Nashville, they were included in the movie *Nashville!*, filmed several years ago, and gained much national publicity.

The only advertising Standard Candy Company does is on the "Grand Ole Opry" radio program every Saturday night. "Grand Ole Opry" is the oldest continuous show in radio. Since 1968, big names in country music have been talking about Goo Goo Cluster on the Goo Goo portion of that program. Roy Acuff, Ernest Tubb, Archie Campbell, Bashful Brother Oswald, the Stoney Mountain Cloggers, Little Jimmy Dickens, Jerry Clower, and Del Wood are numbered among country music fans of Goo Goo Cluster. But you don't have to be a country music fan to go ga ga over a Goo Goo.

Otto Schnering Is My Name, Advertising Is My Game

Probably the first candy man to capitalize fully on the power of advertising was Otto Schnering. In 1923, he chartered an airplane and dropped Baby Ruth candy bars by parachute over the city of Pittsburgh, Pennsylvania.

The Curtiss Candy Company was founded in 1916 in a back room over a plumbing shop on North Halstead Street in Chicago. Schnering, the company's founder, used his mother's maiden name for the firm, figuring that Curtiss was more American-sounding than Schnering. German surnames weren't too popular in the United States during World War I.

According to company records, the Baby Ruth bar first appeared in 1920. The bar, made of a chewy caramel center and peanuts, all covered with chocolate, became a national hit as a five-cent candy bar. Schnering went all out to sell his bar to the folks of America.

The Curtiss Company advertised extensively in magazines like *Collier's*, *The Saturday Evening Post*, and *Open Road for Boys*. Some of the slogans used in ads from the 1920s through the 1950s were:

"The Best Bite of All"
"The Favorite Candy of Over Fifty Million People!"
"Sweetest Story Ever Sold!"
and
"A Friend in Need"

Schnering also launched ad campaigns featuring famous personalities of the times. The Dionne Quintuplets were pictured in ads in which Baby Ruth was stated to be "the *first* and only candy served the Quints, the World's Wonder Children." Dr. Allan Roy Dafoe, their doctor, was quoted in the ads extolling the virtues of Baby Ruth.

The group of child actors who appeared in many slapstick *Our Gang* movies were also featured in Baby Ruth campaigns. The original *Our Gang* kids, who acted in the mid 1920s, were Mary Kornman, Farina, Joe Cobb, Mickey

Daniels, and Jackie Condon, and it was this group that
appeared in the ads for Baby Ruth. (Spanky Macfarland,
Darla Hood, Buckwheat, and others were of a later generation.)

Chances are, the Baby Ruth bar wasn't named after the
baseball player, Babe Ruth, although one reference source
states that Ruth's name was appropriated for the bar without his permission. According to another source, the name
Baby Ruth was supplied by a Mrs. George Williamson. She
supposedly helped develop the formula for the candy bar
and named it in honor of her own granddaughter. This
version probably isn't true, however, because Mr. George
Williamson wasn't president of the Curtiss Candy Company. He headed a rival Chicago firm, the Williamson
Candy Company, which produced Baby Ruth's direct competitor, the Oh Henry! bar.

The commonly accepted story is that the candy bar was
named in honor of a daughter of former President Grover
Cleveland. Ruth Cleveland had been the pet of the nation
when she was an infant. (Ruth was born in 1891. Her
sister, Esther, born in 1893, was the first child of a President to be born in the White House.)

Otto Schnering not only believed in the efficacy of
advertising; he also believed that it was his duty to provide
employment for as many people as he could during the
depths of the Depression in the 1930s. He introduced his
penny Baby Ruth (and also the one-cent version of Butterfinger, which came out in 1926) during the Depression,

"Don't these guys ever eat anything but Baby Ruth?"

Well, Soldier, anywhere and anytime you do "fatigue" duty, you'll think the same . . .

Because wherever our fighters go, Baby Ruth goes too. And so do many other fine foods produced and packaged by Curtiss Candy Company.

Our big food plants are working day and night to keep pace with the demands of the Armed Forces . . . and the home front as well.

Active, hard-working people realize that Baby Ruth and Butterfinger are *great* candy bars, rich in dextrose sugar, providing real food energy to help folks fight fatigue, to carry on their work and play.

While we are not always able to keep all dealers supplied with Baby Ruth and Butterfinger we promise you our best efforts to produce both the quantity you demand and the quality you expect of these great American Candy Bars.

BUY U. S.
WAR BONDS
AND STAMPS

When you don't find
BABY RUTH
*on the candy counter,
remember . . . Uncle
Sam's needs come
first with us as
with you.*

CURTISS CANDY COMPANY • *Producers of Fine Foods* • CHICAGO, ILLINOIS

putting his plants on a round-the-clock basis, with four six-hour shifts, in order to employ the maximum number of workers. The "wrappers," who were young girls, hand-wrapped each of the little penny bars before placing them into boxes. They worked at a steady pace, since they were paid on a "piecework" arrangement. Though the times were bleak, the girls were a happy group, grateful to have jobs that helped put food on the table in those tough times.

More Big Drops

Buoyed by the success of raining Baby Ruth bars on Pittsburgh in 1923, Otto Schnering decided to expand his airplane candy drops to cities in forty states. That campaign not only established Baby Ruth as a national favorite, but it also made a national favorite of another Curtiss product, Butterfinger. The Butterfinger bar, a chocolate-covered honeycombed peanut bar, was included in many of the later drops.

Butterfinger became Curtiss's number two selling bar and was featured alongside Baby Ruth in many ad campaigns. One Butterfinger slogan that was repeated a number of times was "New delight, bite after bite after bite!"

Curtiss products, including Butterfinger, were sponsors of Guy Lombardo and his orchestra on radio in the late 1920s and early thirties. They also accompanied Admiral Richard Byrd to the South Pole in 1928.

Some other Curtiss products of the 1920s and thirties were rolls of Baby Ruth Fruit Drops and Baby Ruth Mints. A number of Curtiss candy bars that were introduced from the 1920s through the 1950s are no longer around today, such as the Peter Pan bar, in its blue, white, and orange wrapper, and the Caramel Nougat. Curtiss also produced a mint patty, but discontinued it after several years.

Cocoanut Grove, a best-selling Curtiss bar for some time, changed its spelling of "cocoanut" to "coconut." The Coconut Grove bar was creamy coconut filling covered with bittersweet chocolate.

An interesting early Curtiss bar was Ostrich Egg. The name was descriptive, because the bar was good-sized and had a somewhat flattened egg shape. Its blue, orange, yellow, and white wrapper gave it a distinctive appearance on candy counters. Some other early Curtiss bars were named Fritzi, Big Bite, I Scream Sandwich, Nickaloaf, Bama, Kandy Kake, and Curtiss Carlton.

Two bars that sold well for a few years in the 1930s and were then phased out were Dip and Buy Jiminy. The Buy Jiminy name was derived from a popular expression of the times; "By Jiminy" meant the same as "Wow," or "You don't say."

Milk Nut Loaf, in a red and white wrapper, carried an interesting slogan: "TOO much for 5¢." Curtiss Nut Roll was a good seller in the 1940s.

After the Curtiss Company became a division of Standard Brands, the parent company also purchased Wayne

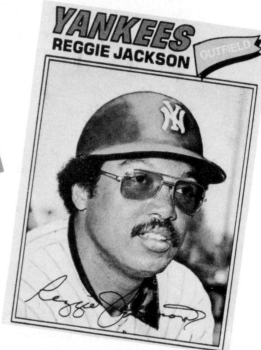

Candies of Fort Wayne, Indiana. An early Wayne product was the Wayne Log, a nut-filled bar. Another popular item in the forties was the Wayne Pecan Caramel bar. What developed into the most popular Wayne candies were the Bun bars, which were either vanilla cream or maple cream peanut clusters.

Another bar, introduced by Curtiss when it was a division of Standard Brands, was — unlike Baby Ruth — named after a baseball player. In 1977, Standard Brands signed an agreement with Reggie Jackson, a baseball superstar who set a record in the World Series of that year. In the last two games of the series the New York Yankees outfielder hit home runs in four consecutive times at bat.

Earlier, when Jackson was with the Baltimore Orioles, he had said, "If I ever played in New York, they'd name a candy bar after me." Sure enough, the bar Reggie! was first produced in 1978, after Jackson's first year — and dramatic World Series — as a Yankee. The wrapper had a picture of Jackson batting; the candy, not really a bar in shape, was a round patty of chocolate-covered caramel and peanuts.

Reggie the baseball player (now with the California Angels) was indeed a superstar; his namesake candy was not, certainly when compared with Baby Ruth and Butterfinger.

As of 1981, when Standard Brands and Nabisco merged to form Nabisco Brands, Inc., Curtiss products have been manufactured by the subsidiary, Nabisco Confections, Inc. In 1982, Nabisco Brands, Inc., divested itself of the Wayne bars and the Reggie bar, which it sold to Storck USA, Inc., makers of Toffifay and other products. Nabisco Confections, Inc., will keep two of Otto Schnering's Curtiss gifts to the candy world front and center, however: Baby Ruth and Butterfinger.

Whiz, Best Nickel Bar There Wuz

One of the more effective advertising slogans in the candy bar business was originated in Bloomington, Illinois, back in the 1930s.

Paul F. Beich (pronounced *bike*) bought a candy manufacturing business that had been started by J. L. Timmerman and John L. Green in 1871. In 1900, Beich and a partner purchased the Lancaster Caramel Company plant in Bloomington from Milton S. Hershey when he decided to get out of the caramel business and concentrate on chocolate products. Caramels in this plant were then made under the name Bloomington Caramel Company.

In 1926, Paul Beich introduced his Whiz Bar, which really wasn't a bar, since it was round. The Whiz Bar consisted of peanuts, marshmallow, and fudge, all covered with dark chocolate. In the first production lines manufacturing the Whiz Bar, the bars were hand-wrapped, but in 1943, automatic wrapping machines were installed in the Beich plant.

When the Whiz Bar was introduced in the middle 1920s, it sold for ten cents. In Depression years the price dropped to five cents. After World War II the price went back up to a dime. And when the bar went out of production in 1972, the price was fifteen cents, and the shape was rec-

tangular. The demise of the bar was due not to a dearth of satisfied customers, but to a lack of modern assembly-line equipment.

In the 1930s the slogan "Whiz, best nickel candy there iz-z!" was coined. When the price of the bar doubled after World War II, the slogan was changed to "Whiz — best candy bar there iz-z!"

Both slogans were popular expressions for many years. As a result, sales of Whiz Bars really put Bloomington on the map.

The Paul F. Beich Company is still around and is doing quite well in the candy business, with items like Katydids and Kathryn Beich Confections, among other products. For a while after the phasing-out of the Whiz Bar, the Beich company produced Whiz Sweet and Salty Peanuts to keep the Whiz trademark alive. The company also manufactured a nut-roll bar called Dipsy Doodle (named after a popular tune in 1937), and Pecan Pete, which was popular in the 1940s. North Star and Frosted Fudge were also old Beich bar items.

For those of us who can remember, the Beich Company is a part of Americana because of Whiz, the best nickel bar there wuz.

Shakespeare and the American Candy Bar

What's the connection between William Shakespeare and an American candy bar? Here's the story.

Donley Cross was a Shakespearean actor performing the Bard's works before audiences in San Francisco in the early 1900s. During one performance, Cross fell off the stage, injuring his back. The injury curtailed Cross's career as a thespian, but since he was an entrepreneur, he looked for other fields to conquer.

In collaboration with Charlie Fox, Cross opened the Fox-Cross Candy Company in Emeryville, across the bay from San Francisco, in 1920. One of the company's first products was a candy bar known as Nu Chu.

The bar that was to make the company famous, however, wasn't launched until 1922. It was named after a dance craze in full swing at the time — and so came to be the famous Charleston Chew! It was made of vanilla-flavored nougat covered with milk chocolate.

The Fox-Cross Candy Company and its popular bar, Charleston Chew!, began to move east into the Chicago area and then the Boston area. Ownership of the product line changed several times over the years, too. The present

owner of the Charleston Chew! bar company is Nabisco Confections, Inc., in Cambridge, Massachusetts. But the candy bar itself is still manufactured in Everett, Massachusetts, where the Fox-Cross Candy Company settled in 1958.

In 1955, Nathan Sloane became the president of Fox-Cross, and in the fall of 1958 he was responsible for introducing Strawberry Charleston Chew! and Chocolate Charleston Chew!, instant successes.

Some candy bars introduced by Fox-Cross were around for only a few years. Chewy-Louie and Astro-Nut (chocolate, nougat, and nuts) were two. By sending in three Astro-Nut wrappers and fifteen cents, you could get an astronaut ring! Twist O'Lemon, a chocolate-covered lemon-flavored nougat bar, was also around for only a few years.

Charleston Chew! was one of the early bars to capitalize on the use of freezer compartments in refrigerators as candy bar depositories. As it says on present-day Charleston Chew! bars, "For a delicious treat . . . chill or freeze Charleston Chew! candy bars . . . then remove a bar from refrigerator . . . place wrapped bar in palm of hand and strike against hard surface . . . remove wrapper and you now have a number of BITE SIZE PIECES ready-to-eat!" Many a Charleston Chew! lover has put that process to good use.

First launched as a five-cent bar in the 1920s, Charleston Chew! is still going strong today, but at a somewhat higher price. The shape of the bar has changed a bit over the years, but the delectable ingredients taste just as great as they did over fifty years ago.

Of All Places, English Toffee in Downstate Illinois

The formula for Heath's English toffee candy was developed in 1928 by a retired Illinois schoolteacher. Four years later, L. S. Heath tried out his formula on a huge scale. The Heath Bar, toffee covered with milk chocolate, was introduced to a national market in 1932, right in the middle of the Depression. Most candy companies were producing four-ounce bars that sold for a nickel each, but the Heath Bar weighed only one ounce, and the experts were skeptical that this bar would ever make it off the launching pad. In fact, many people thought it was just a penny candy, since it was similar in size to many of the popular penny items available at the time.

When the Heath Bar first came out, people not familiar with the Heath family name called the bar the H and H Bar. Those people thought they were reading the word "eat" between the two big H's (HeatH), and that this was just part of the package sell.

Some of the prospective jobbers even looked at the small bar and asked, "What is that thing, a laxative?" Indeed, a popular laxative, Ex-Lax, was at that time available in a similar-size package.

The experts were proven wrong about the Heath Bar, though. Sales rose until the bar became one of the most popular candies in the country. The price increased over the years, and the weight of the bar has fluctuated, but the Heath Bar is still found, nationwide, to satisfy the craving of chocolate-covered toffee addicts.

Some other bars produced by the L. S. Heath Company, Inc., located in Robinson, Illinois, are Little Heath Bars,

Heath Milk Chocolate, Heath Milk Chocolate Toffee Crunch, Heath Milk Chocolate with Peanuts, and Heath Milk Chocolate with Natural Cereal and Raisins.

A division of Heath is Fenn Brothers, Inc., located in Belmont, California, which now manufactures only hard ground candy (butter brickle, toffee, peppermint, and such) for use in ice cream. The company was founded by Henry Fenn in 1898 in Sioux Falls, South Dakota. In the 1940s, Fenn Brothers made several candy bars, perhaps the most popular of which was Woodward's Butter Brickle, an English toffee–style bar. Other Fenn favorites were Fenn's Cherry Baby Bogie (peanuts, chocolate, and cherry fondant), and Fenn's Walnut Crush. The latter bar was considered unusual, because walnuts rather than the more popular peanuts were at the heart of the bar.

The Pony Express and George Washington Chase

St. Joseph, Missouri, was on one end of the two-thousand-mile Pony Express route, which lasted little more than a year and a half at the start of the 1860s. George Washington Chase, who came to St. Joseph in 1871, lasted for quite a while longer. He came to St. Joseph to practice medicine, but shortly found that selling groceries and produce was a much more profitable venture.

In 1876, his teen-age son convinced Chase to bring two candy experts in from the East. The idea was to set up a candy factory on the second floor of the store. The idea worked, and confections were turned out in abundance.

After the turn of the century the Chases developed and marketed the first candy bar to be made west of the Mississippi River. The bar, named Cherry Chase, consisted of a quarter-pound mound of chopped peanuts and chocolate with a center of cherry fondant. It sold for the big price of five cents. In later years the Chase Candy Company put into production a smaller version of the Cherry Chase.

That bar, Cherry Mash, became, and is to this day, the company's best seller. Distributed throughout only an eight-state area, it is the largest-selling candy bar of its type in the United States.

In the 1940s, the Chase Company marketed Chase's Toasted Nut Candy Bar and Chase's Brunch Candy Bar. The word *brunch* first appeared in an American dictionary in 1934. Meaning a meal combining the elements of breakfast and lunch, the word was a good name for a candy bar.

The Chase Candy Company now shares facilities in a factory with the Poe Candy Company in St. Joseph (Chase & Poe Candy Companies). And at that factory, production of the Cherry Mash just keeps rolling along to satisfy demands of the buying public.

Halajian, Kazanjian, Shamlian, Hagopian, Kazanjian, and Chouljian

Halajian, Kazanjian, Shamlian, Hagopian, Kazanjian, and Chouljian was not the name of a law firm. You went to these fellows in 1919 to buy some candy.

Peter Paul Halajian, already a candy maker, decided to form a company for producing and selling candy on a large scale. He was joined by five friends to form Peter Paul Candies.

The original business was located in a loft in New Haven, Connecticut, in 1919. By 1922, the company had relocated in Naugatuck, where its headquarters still are.

The first Peter Paul candy bar was the Konabar, introduced in 1919. The bar was a blend of coconut, fruits, nuts, and chocolate. The bar that was to make Peter Paul famous, however, wasn't introduced until 1922; this was the Mounds bar. Coconut and bittersweet (now called dark) chocolate were the ingredients then, just as they are today. It isn't documented as to how the name Mounds was chosen.

The first Mounds wrappers contained only a single bar and sold for five cents. During the Depression, Peter Paul management made an interesting move. The size of the Mounds package was doubled, but still sold for only a nickel. Putting two bars into one package was a smart marketing move, and business increased, in spite of the hard times. Peter Paul also converted a soap-wrapping machine to handle candy bars, and used the machinery to replace hand-wrapping. Switching from a foil wrap to cellophane was also done at this time.

Peter Paul was a pioneer in radio advertising, sponsoring such well-known newscasters as Gabriel Heatter ("Ah, there's good news tonight!"), Edwin C. Hill ("The human side of the news"), and Bill Slater during the late 1920s and the thirties. The slogan "What a bar of candy for five cents" became the nationwide pitch for Mounds.

In 1934, the Dreams bar was introduced; it had the same coconut filling as Mounds but was covered with milk chocolate instead of bittersweet. The Dreams bar remained in production until 1948 and was better liked by kids, but adults favored Mounds. Smile-a-While was a chocolate-covered coconut double bar that sold well for a while in the 1950s.

Peter Paul entered the TV advertising market in the mid-1950s. The Peter Paul Pixies, cartoon characters, made the two words "Indescribably Delicious" a saying that captured the imagination of a nation. Kids especially liked to roll the syllables of those two words off their tongues. It was this campaign that really made the name Mounds a household word.

Joy to the World

Peter Paul had found a good thing in coconut as an ingredient of candy bars. In 1948 the company came across another ingredient that was going to boost sales for the company, the almond. It was in that year that the Almond Joy was born. With just a bit of restructuring, the Dreams bar, only mildly successful, was turned into a winner. Whole roasted almonds were added to a coconut center, covered with milk chocolate, and *voilà!* Almond Joy. An advertising slogan that helped make the bar really stick in people's minds was "Oh Boy! Almond Joy!" The bar sold for ten cents when it was first introduced, because of the high costs of goods in the aftermath of World War II, but the price didn't keep appreciative fans from buying this new taste treat.

Almond Cluster was the second Peter Paul product to contain almonds. It came on the scene in 1959, and was produced in the Salinas, California, Peter Paul plant for West Coast sales, but it was soon distributed nationally. For Almond Cluster, the almonds were diced, added to malted milk crunch, and covered with milk chocolate. Almond Cluster is no longer being produced, but, along with the still popular Almond Joy, it helped establish the almond, alongside the coconut, as a top ingredient of Peter Paul candies.

Carmen Miranda, the Brazilian Bombshell

Carmen Miranda was a singer known as the Brazilian Bombshell. Wearing elaborate dresses and huge headdresses laden with fruit, she appeared in numerous movies in the 1940s and early 1950s. What did Carmen Miranda have to do with a candy bar? Nothing. But something else from Brazil did: the Brazil nut.

After a bit of research and development, the Peter Paul Company came up with a new bar in 1965 called Caravelle, a combination of soft caramel, crisped rice, milk chocolate, and Brazil nuts.

In 1972, Peter Paul picked on the peanut for a new bar, Peanut Butter with No Jelly. Milk chocolate covered a soft peanut butter center laced with crisp bits of rice. That bar is no longer being produced.

The Star Bar was launched in 1978, with the peanut again as the main feature. Peanuts and soft peanut nougat were wrapped in caramel and chocolate.

In 1972, Peter Paul acquired the York Peppermint Pattie. A silver and blue wrapper surrounded a specially "grained" or textured mint patty center enrobed in chocolate. When Peter Paul acquired the patty, it was distributed only in the East. By 1976 it was distributed nationwide.

Today, the company started by Peter Paul Halajian is known as Peter Paul Cadbury, Inc. It manufactures such Cadbury bar products as Cadbury's Milk Chocolate, Cadbury's Hazel Nut, Cadbury's Caramello, Cadbury's Fruit and Nut, Cadbury's Almond, Cadbury's Brazil Nut, and Cadbury's Krisp.

Is That a Mammoth? No, Just a PowerHouse

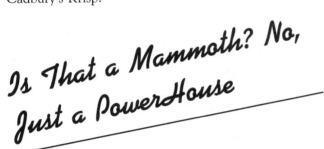

B ack in the late 1930s and early 1940s, almost every community had a drug store that served as a hangout for kids. The gang of four I ran around with in Evanston, Illinois, had its meeting place in Spencer's Drug Store. It was a mom and pop drug store, presided over by a great favorite of all the kids, "Doc" Spencer.

After many a ball game we'd spend our thirst nickel there on the best drink bargain of the times, a bottle of Double Cola. If each of us had an extra nickel for a candy bar, the choice was hard, because there were so many great bars to choose from. But if there was just one nickel for candy to divide among the four of us, the choice was easy. We just went ahead and bought a PowerHouse.

A PowerHouse bar back in those days was a four-ounce bar known as a nut roll, which broke into four good-sized pieces and was enough to provide each of us with a good mouthful of candy to chew. PowerHouse had an interior of peanuts, fudge, and caramel, and was enrobed in chocolate.

The company that produced this mammoth bar was the Walter H. Johnson Candy Company. In the 1940s, the Johnson Company sponsored a series of ads on the comic pages of many Sunday newspapers. A cartoon character, Roger Wilco, was the hero of adventures for PowerHouse. Any kid who sent in fifteen cents and a wrapper from a PowerHouse bar got an "exciting scientific Roger Wilco Magni-Ray Ring!"

In 1966, the Johnson Company became part of Peter Paul Candies. There are no records of the Johnson Company relating to PowerHouse, so there is no official launch date for the bar. It probably first appeared in the late 1920s. Another product of the company was Big Bonus, a somewhat smaller bar than PowerHouse.

PowerHouse is still around to tickle taste buds. It's now packaged in similar fashion to other Peter Paul products. It's no longer the mammoth of bars, but it still packs a real taste wallop!

Gladys and the Dirty Old Man

One of the most popular TV shows in the late 1960s and early 1970s was "Rowan and Martin's Laugh-In." Many catch phrases from this program became

national by-words: "Sock it to me"; "Look that up in your Funk and Wagnalls"; "Beautiful downtown Burbank"; "Verrry interesting!"; "Here come de judge"; "You bet your sweet bippy"; "Do you want a Walnetto?" This last phrase actually brought a candy product out of retirement.

Walnettos, originally produced by the J. N. Collins Company in the early 1920s, were individually wrapped chews made of hard caramel containing walnut bits. Originally sold as penny candies, Walnettos were then put into packets that sold for a nickel.

Walnettos were popular with kids because they were long-lasting, and the kids thought they were getting their money's worth. Walnettos dropped off in sales, however, and finally the Collins Company was taken over by Peter Paul Candies in 1929. Walnettos sales picked up when the new owners began a media-marketing campaign.

Walnettos sponsored one of the more popular children's radio programs of the 1930s, "Uncle Don." Uncle Don was to radio almost what Captain Kangaroo was to TV in later years. He usually started off the program by singing his famed "Hibbidy Gits" song, which began:

> Hello nephews, nieces too,
> Mothers and daddies, how are you?
> This is Uncle Don all set to go
> With a meeting on the ra-di-o.

The song concluded with a series of nonsense words, starting with "Hibbidy gits."

Uncle Don was portrayed by Don Carney, and his program helped sell many a packet of Walnettos. One story that made the rounds was that Carney, signing off one night, thought that the microphone was off, and said, "There! I guess that'll hold the little bastards for another night!"

When Walnettos' sales again dropped in the 1960s, the product was put into partial retirement, but was resurrected when the name was given recognition by Gladys and the dirty old man on "Laugh-In."

Ruth Buzzi played the part of Gladys, a spinsterish lady with an umbrella, who was forever whacking the "dirty old man," portrayed by Arte Johnson, as he tried to snuggle up to her on a park bench. It was one of Arte Johnson's catch phrases, "Do you want a Walnetto?" said with a leer, that resulted in his being whacked with the umbrella so that he often slid off the park bench.

A few years after the demise of the TV show, Walnettos were retired for good.

What Comes from Pittsburgh Besides Pirates?

David L. Clark opened his small candy business in Pittsburgh in 1886. He did the manufacturing, selling, delivering, and bookkeeping. By 1917, when the United States entered World War I, the D. L. Clark Company was making many types of candies. Soldiers liked and wanted candy, so that year David Clark came out with his first five-cent candy bar. It was originally called simply Clark, but it was the same bar we know today as the Clark bar. The ingredients, honeycombed ground roasted peanuts, covered with milk chocolate, became a favorite as soon as Clark hit the marketplace.

Chewing gum was also made at the time by the Clark Company. In the 1920s Clark wrappers were printed up as certificates that could be turned in for free packages of Clark's gum. The legend on the Clark wrappers read: "Send 15 of these certificates and receive by parcel post 3

5¢ packages of Clark's fine chewing gum consisting of 1 package each — Clark's Teaberry, Peppermint and Sweetwood gum."

Another legend on the same wrapper read: "Try eating a Clark bar every day between 2 & 4 P.M. Drink a glass of water and see how much pep you have when the day is done."

A companion best-selling bar was introduced by Clark in 1930. Zagnut consisted of peanut-butter crunch covered with toasted coconut.

Clark's Crispy Bar came out in 1977, and in 1979 Clark's Nutcracker Bar was first manufactured. Sunpower, intro-

Do these kids really care i
Clark is number one in 15¢ b

Probably not. They just like Clark and Zagnut bars. So much, in fact, they've made Clark the number one 15¢ candy bar for the second straight year in the 1973 Candy Marketer National Bar Survey. And Zagnut now ranks 3rd, up from 6th.

The popularity of Clark goes quite a way. Clark ranked

high on the national surve and fun-size. And Clark among the leaders in th

Clark's the candy b they like find wh Zagnut

The D.L Pittsbur

The Center of Attraction

For delicious flavor the Clark Candy Bar is in a class by itself. That's because the center of this world-famous candy bar is blended by a special interweaving process from luscious caramel and fresh peanut butter. It's a real "center of attraction," covered with thick, rich, palate-pleasing milk chocolate!

Ask your dealer for the Clark Candy Bar. Only a nickel wherever you are.

THE CENTER OF ATTRACTION

ALL OVER THE WORLD

FOR QUICK ENERGY, EAT A CLARK BAR WITH A GLASS OF WATER BETWEEN 2 AND 4 P. M.

duced in 1980, is made with sunflower seeds and nuts. Dutch Treat and Granola Twins were also introduced in 1980.

Other early Clark bars popular in their day but no longer being manufactured were the Honest Square bar, the Coconut Bar, the Iceland Sandwich, the Yellow Gold bar, and the Light and Clarconut bars.

The D. L. Clark Company became part of the Beatrice Foods Company in 1955, and in 1978 merged with the M. J. Holloway Company, but Pittsburgh is still headquarters for the Clark Company. So it's really true that things other than Pirates come from Pittsburgh. The Clark bar and the many other Clark products are ample proof.

Just for the Record Books

What's the largest candy bar ever ever made? A giant Clark bar, billed as the "Largest Candy Bar in the World," was presented in 1981 at an amusement park near the home of the D. L. Clark Company. The bar weighed in at 3100 pounds (beating its one-ton goal), was

15 feet long and 20 inches thick. The biggie bar amounted to the equivalent of about 19,000 regular-size Clark bars.

After the presentation, the giant bar was served in small pieces to the crowd. Small donations were accepted for the pieces, and the money was later contributed to a local charity.

A tip of the hat to the Clark bar for setting the record. It couldn't happen to a nicer bar.

Hip Hip Hooray for Holloway

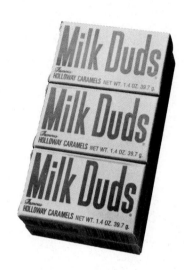

One of the neat things for me about going to junior high school in Evanston, Illinois, in the 1930s was having a friend whose dad ran a candy company in Chicago. My friend's dad made one of my very favorite candies at the time, Holloway's Milk Duds. Milk Duds were small, marble-sized vanilla-flavored chewy caramels covered with milk chocolate, and they came in yellow boxes with brown lettering. They were always tasty, and they seemed especially so whenever my friend would bring a fresh box for sampling purposes.

Milton J. Holloway took over F. Hoffman & Company of Chicago in 1920. One of Mr. Holloway's new products was a nut roll he called Sweet Sixteen. This was one of the first five-cent nut roll bars produced and sold in the United States. Sweet Sixteen is no longer made, but it caused quite a stir in the marketplace when it appeared on the scene.

Holloway Milk Duds and a caramel sucker called Slo Poke were introduced in 1926. Slo Poke became a real favorite with kids, because it seemed as if that vanilla-flavored caramel sucker lasted all day.

Many kids, in fact, used to lick awhile, then put the sucker back inside the wrapper for deposit in a back pocket until the licking urge took over again.

Black Cow, a caramel sucker with a chocolate-flavored covering, was introduced to the market shortly after Milk Duds and Slo Poke. Another early favorite was Baby Holloway's. A bar containing pecans, Trade Wind, was popular in the 1940s, as was a Holloway's Caramel Candy Sucker.

In 1960 the Holloway Company was sold to Beatrice Foods Company and then was merged with the D. L. Clark Company, under whose name such old Holloway products as Milk Duds, Slo Poke, and Black Cow are still being made. New items are Alligator Eggs (1979), Apple Caramels (1979), and Wildfire (1980).

The Holloway name no longer appears on Milk Duds or Slo Poke, but the terrific taste of the products remains the same.

Leo Hirshfield's Daughter

Leo Hirshfield was looking around for a name for the new confection he was making from a recipe he'd brought over from Europe. It was the year 1896, and Hirshfield's thoughts wandered to his six-year-old daughter, Clara, nicknamed Tootsie. It didn't take Hirshfield long to realize he'd found the name for his product: Tootsie Roll!

Hirshfield's candy was round, chewy, and chocolatey, and today's Tootsie Roll still looks and tastes pretty much as it did when first introduced over eighty years ago.

Tootsie Rolls were the first penny candy to be individually wrapped in paper, and were one of the top choices of kids who had a few pennies to spend on satisfying a sweet tooth.

Hirshfield's business started in New York, but over the years business boomed, and moves were made to larger and larger quarters. The headquarters for Tootsie Rolls is now in Chicago.

In the 1930s, the first soft-centered lollipops, Tootsie Pops, were sold. The hard candy on the outside covered the Tootsie Roll center.

During World War II, Tootsie Rolls were favored by soldiers because they could be kept in pockets and barracks bags and didn't melt. They were also a great source of quick energy. In the late 1940s, Tootsie Rolls were advertised on the comic pages of many Sunday newspapers. The feature cartoon character was Captain Tootsie (a kind of Superman), who took kids on various adventures, such as viewing the filming of the movie *The Babe Ruth Story*, starring William Bendix as the Babe.

Tootsie Rolls are nationally known, and are the favorite candy of a number of famous people. Some show business personalities who have been linked with Tootsie Rolls are Frank Sinatra and Sammy Davis, Jr. Several years ago when Sammy Davis, Jr., was performing in the hit production, Candy Man, he'd distribute Tootsie Rolls to the audience. And it has been reported that Frank Sinatra doesn't perform in a city unless a supply of Tootsie Rolls is ready and waiting in his room.

The Tootsie Roll is indeed a part of Americana, and will continue to be a favorite of each new generation of kids. To make sure that the appetites of Tootsie Roll and Tootsie Pops lovers are satisfied, a good number of each are produced on a daily basis. Every day about six million Tootsie Pops are manufactured, and about ten million Tootsie Rolls!

Patty and Dot and Taffy, Etc.

In 1864, Ernest Von Au and Joseph Maison founded the company with the product name Mason. Mason's Black Crows were born in the 1890s. The product was originally to be called Black Rose, but when the name was given orally to a printer, he heard the name as Black Crows, and so printed up wrappers with that name on them. The wrappers were used, and the name stuck. Still produced, this item is now called Mason Licorice Crows. Other products of the company were Mason Mints, Mason Dots, Mason Spice Berries, and Mason Cherry Dots. A popular Mason candy bar of the 1940s was the Rum-or bar.

I spied on Junior to learn the truth about candy!

DO AS CHILDREN DO! EAT TOOTSIE ROLLS—THE LUSCIOUS CANDY THAT HELPS BEAT FATIGUE!

● Kids are smart—they know their candy! Grown-ups who want to be more like tireless youngsters should do what kids do—eat plenty of chewy chocolaty Tootsie Rolls.

Made with milk, enriched with dextrose, Tootsie Rolls are *packed* with energy. A 5¢ Tootsie Roll contains as many energy units as a woman uses doing nearly two hours of ironing.

Try Tootsie Rolls in lunch boxes, for extra-quick desserts, bridge party refreshments. Take a tip from Junior. Get a *Tootsie Roll* today!

Tootsie Rolls Co. also makes these other fine food products

TOOTSIE FUDGE
TOOTSIE POPS
TOOTSIE TEMPTEES
TOOTSIE CARAMELS
TOOTSIE V-M*

*Vitamin-Mineral fortifier that makes milk taste like Tootsie Rolls.

BUY WAR BONDS AND STAMPS

Tootsie Rolls

★ Still only 1¢ and 5¢

Popular bars in the 1950s were Peaks, Queens, Mason Milk Chocolate Pecan Cocoanut, and Mason Chocolate Cocoanut.

Albert J. Bonomo and his son Victor, whose company was founded in 1897, manufactured many fine candies, including the Thanks Bar and Hats Off. The Bonomo Company's most famous product was Bonomo's Turkish Taffy.

Both Mason and Bonomo are now a part of Tootsie Roll Industries, Inc. In 1979, the company came out with its first entry in the chocolate-coated product field. That's when the Mason Mint Patty came off the production line as the Tootsie Mason Mint Patty.

A Snicker Is a Slightly Stifled Laugh

What's been the number one favorite candy bar of Americans for many years? Snickers. Today, Snickers consists of peanuts in caramel, on top of peanut-butter nougat, all covered with milk chocolate. When the bar first appeared, however, it didn't have a chocolate coating.

Frank C. Mars and his wife began making candy in the kitchen of their home in Tacoma, Washington, back in 1911. The Mars family moved to larger quarters in Minneapolis, Minnesota, in 1920. That's where Frank's first candy bar was manufactured. It was called the Mar-O-Bar, but it didn't set the buying public on fire by any means, so it was allowed to fall by the wayside.

The company name, Mar-O-Bar Company, was changed, in 1926, to Mars Candies. The company moved to a new plant in the Chicago area in 1929, and it was in this plant in 1930 that the chocolate-covered Snickers bar was born.

Over fifty years later, Snickers leads all candy bars in nationwide sales. Here's one bar that can truly claim to be called the Great American Candy Bar!

Athos, Porthos, and Aramis

Alexandre Dumas's best-known novel, *The Three Musketeers*, appeared in 1844. Athos, Porthos, and Aramis, the three heroes in the title, and their friend d'Artagnan appeared in several other Dumas novels, as well. The musketeers were gentlemen in the service of the kings of France, and, as Dumas tells it, had all kinds of brave and bold adventures.

About a hundred years later, in 1932, the Mars Company began the manufacture of a new candy bar bearing the name of Dumas's novel. Instead of the number three being spelled out, however, the numeral 3 was used, so the bar's name was "3 Musketeers Bar." This bar caused quite a stir among kids of the 1930s, because it actually consisted of three bars in one wrapper for just a nickel. Each of the three was covered with milk chocolate. The interior of one was a fluffy vanilla nougat, the second a fluffy chocolate nougat, and the third a strawberry-flavored nougat.

The 3 Musketeers candy bar has changed over the years. It's now an elongated single bar, with a center of fluffy chocolate nougat. But, whatever its ingredients, 3 Musketeers remains as popular as ever.

A Galaxy Is Where Buck Rogers and Flash Gordon Play

Our solar system consists of the sun, nine planets, about forty-nine moons (at last count), countless asteroids, and occasional visiting comets, such as Halley's. To those of us on Earth this is a big system, but it's small potatoes compared with a galaxy. A galaxy contains an average of a hundred billion solar masses, and the diameter of a galaxy is mind-boggling.

Our solar system is part of the galaxy called the Milky Way. That part of the Milky Way visible from Earth is seen as a luminous band in the night sky and is truly an impressive sight.

The Milky Way candy bar was an instant success on this planet. Frank C. Mars introduced the bar into our galaxy in 1923, and this new bar of chocolate-flavored nougat, topped with caramel and covered with chocolate, has been a stellar seller ever since.

HEY JOE, LOOK WHAT AUNT MARY SENT ME...

AND DO I LOVE MILKY WAYS !

Yes, aunts and uncles, mothers and fathers, sweethearts and wives all over the country are sending delicious Milky Way candy bars. They know their boys will thrill to the taste of the delightful pure milk chocolate coating, the smooth creamy caramel and the luscious chocolate nougat center flavored with real malted milk . . . a taste treat found only in a Milky Way. Just think what a whole box of delicious Milky Ways would mean to your boy now!

Mighty and Marvelous

Forrest E. Mars, Sr., son of Frank C. Mars, founded M&M Limited in Newark, New Jersey. It was at this confectionery plant that M&M's Plain Chocolate Candies were introduced in 1941. Forrest's business associate was named Bruce Murrie, and the name M&M's was derived from the joining of Mars and Murrie.

When American servicemen in World War II got hold of this new candy treat, they quickly found it could withstand extremes in climate because of its unique sugar-coated shell. The new candy became extremely popular as a quick-energy provider.

In 1954, M&M's Peanut Chocolate Candies were introduced and also became an immediate success. The company made its move from Newark to a new plant in Hackettstown, New Jersey, where the headquarters for what is now known as M&M/Mars, a Division of Mars, Inc., is located.

To this day both the plain and peanut M&M's are identified by the M on their sugar-coated shells. The advertising slogan "The Milk Chocolate Melts in Your Mouth — Not in Your Hand" has become one of the classic slogans of candy lore.

An Almond by Any Other Name Is Still an Almond

One of the highlights in the life of any kid living in the Chicago area in the 1930s was a visit to the Mars Candies plant. That's when visions of candy bars dancing in your head became reality. During the plant tour you saw all your favorites — Snickers, Milky Way, and 3 Musketeers. You might even have seen some not-so-favor-

It's here...the New
MARS
Cocoanut Bar
that your customers are waiting for

MARS Cocoanut Bar 5¢

5¢

It's the candy bar you've been waiting for, too . . . it's the candy bar
your customers want! It's the luscious, new five cent MARS
COCOANUT BAR.

Powerful newspaper and television

The
Dr. I.Q.
Candy Bar is a
delicious treat of nougat,
and smooth rich caramel,
roasted peanuts, all covered
with finest milk chocolate.

You will enjoy
an assort-
of Mars

When you crave good Candy
eat
A Mars Confection
MFD. BY
MARS Inc. Chicago, Ill.

Have you tried
the delicious
flavors of
The 3 MUSKETEERS

Dr. I.Q.
REG. U.S. PAT. OFF.   NET. WT. 1¾ OZ.   5¢

Dr. I.Q.

"The Answer to Your Taste Question"

—SWEET MILK CHOCOLATE, PEANUTS,

SYRUP, MILK CONDENSED WITH
TABLE OIL, WHITES OF EGGS, SALT.

INCORPORATED

The Dr. I.Q. Candy
Bar is made in our
ideal modern sunlit candy kitchens
and is as pure as it is good.
MFD. BY
MARS Inc. Chicago, Ill.

4201105-1
BEST BEFORE
DEC 01
1763

GUARANTEE OF SATISFACTION
Your MARS Bar should be fresh and in good condition. If not, we will replace it.
Just return the unused portion and tell us where and when you bought it.

NUTRITION INFORMATION PER SERVING
SERVING SIZE: 1 BAR
CALORIES 210 PROTEIN 3 GRAMS CARBOHYDRATE 27 GRAMS FAT 10 GRAMS
PERCENTAGE OF U.S. RECOMMENDED DAILY ALLOWANCES (U.S. RDA)
PROTEIN 4 THIAMINE 2 CALCIUM 2
RIBOFLAVIN .. 6 VITAMIN C .. 4 IRON 2
NIACIN ...... 5 VITAMIN A ..*
*CONTAINS LESS THAN 2 PERCENT OF THE U.S. RDA OF THESE NUTRIENTS

Mars
BAR
Mars
BAR
NET WT 1.52 OZ. 43 g
Crunchy Nuts,
Caramel & Nougat
in Milk Chocolate

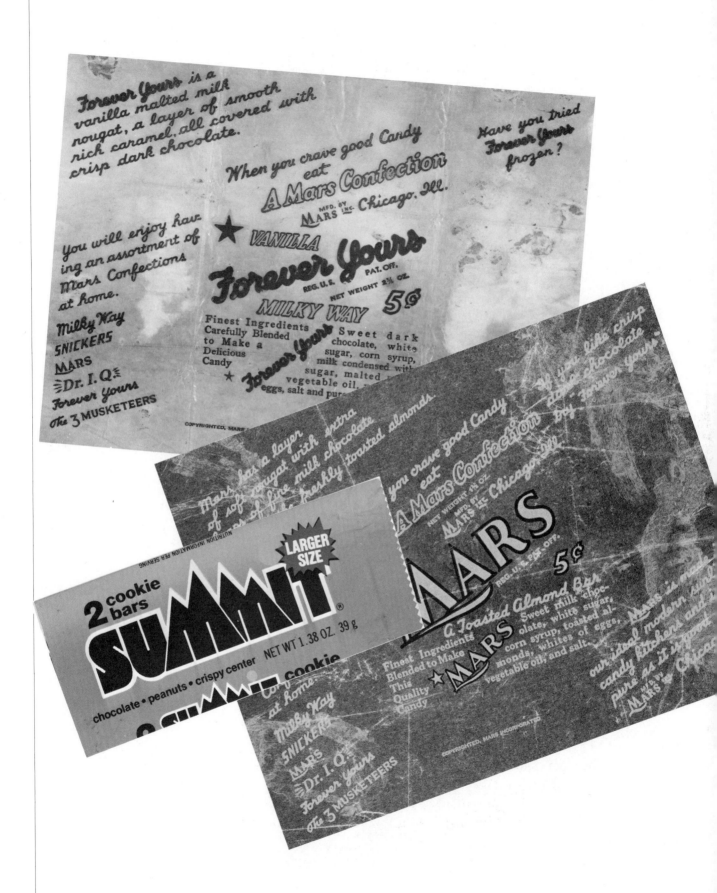

59

ite bars for kids, Forever Yours, coming off the production line. Forever Yours was subtitled "The Vanilla Milky Way." It had a nougat center topped with caramel, but was covered with a dark chocolate rather than the milk chocolate that surrounded a Milky Way. Some other bars produced by Mars Candies at the time were Honey Almond, Thrills, and Two Bits.

If you happened to be visiting the Mars plant in 1936, you saw a new product coming off the production line. That was the Mars Almond Bar, today known just as the Mars Bar. Vanilla-flavored nougat was topped with whole roasted almonds and then covered with a thick milk chocolate. The wrapper design and colors have changed over the years, but the bar still has the same great taste it had back in 1936.

Two bars produced by the company that were relatively popular in the 1940s, but are no longer made, were Ping and Dr. I.Q. The Ping candy bar, covered with dark chocolate, had a white nougat center with walnuts.

The Dr. I.Q. candy bar consisted of nougat, caramel, and peanuts covered with milk chocolate. A popular radio program, "Dr. I.Q.," aired from 1939 to 1950. Dr. I.Q. gave away silver dollars to those who could answer his questions. The programs were staged in movie houses around the country, and roving microphones were used by assistants who moved around in the audience looking for contestants. The most famous phrase to come out of that program was "I have a lady in the balcony, Doctor." In the show's first year, $700 a week was budgeted for the silver-dollar winners by Mars Inc., the sponsor. Losers received a box of the sponsor's candy bars.

"Howdy Doody," a popular children's television show, made a real push for the Mars Cocoanut Bar in the early 1950s. The show sold a lot of kids on the five-cent bar before they even had a chance to see it in the marketplace.

The M&M/Mars Company has marketed several new products in recent years. Starburst Fruit Chews came out in 1976. The Summit, a cookie bar, is another new product, and the package is an interesting one. The two m's in the word Summit are drawn on the wrapper to look like mountains. They also represent the two m's in M&M's. Summit was introduced in 1977; it's made of chopped peanuts on top of cream-filled crisp wafers covered with chocolate.

Also launched in 1977 was the Twix Cookie Bars package. Each Twix consists of creamy caramel and a crunchy cookie covered with milk chocolate.

It's highly probable that in coming years other delectable candy products will emerge from the kitchens of M&M/Mars.

Beware of a Greek Bearing Gifts?

In 1974, the Snack-master Division of M&M/Mars thought Marathon would be a good name for their new candy bar. The name goes back to 490 B.C., when the Greeks and Persians were having a tiff in Marathon, Greece. The Greek forces emerged victorious from battle, and the news of the victory was carried to Athens by a long-distance runner. The runner covered approximately twenty-five miles in that jaunt, and the word *marathon* has been applied to a long-distance race that tasks the runner's endurance.

The Marathon candy bar consists of twisted ropes of caramel covered with milk chocolate. The name choice was based on the long size of the bar and its long-lasting characteristics.

The same division launched Skittles Fruit Chews in 1973, and Munch Peanut Bar in 1971. Munch is a bar of well-roasted peanuts with a crunchy, buttery candy base. Many people have found it a treat to crunch on a Munch after lunch.

Did You Drink It? No, You Ate It

In the 1930s, the Trudeau Candy Company of St. Paul, Minnesota, created the Seven Up candy bar. It consisted of little individual candy segments, each with a different center; the whole bar was covered with dark chocolate. It originally had one segment containing a Brazil nut, another with jelly, and one with coconut, and the other four had different kinds of caramel fillings. In the 1940s, the Seven Up bar, with its seven little units, was a popular seller in the Midwestern states. Another popular Trudeau bar of the times was the Pep Up bar.

The Trudeau Company was purchased by the Pearson Candy Company in 1951, and that company continued to manufacture the dark chocolate Seven Up, together with

a milk chocolate–covered version. The Pearson Candy Company produced other bars, too. One of them, Choo Choo, was a popular salted nut roll of the 1940s. (A present good seller is Pearson's Salted Nut Roll.)

During the 1960s, the Seven Up bar was changed in shape, and the Brazil nut was eliminated. The interior flavors also changed over the years. When the bar was last produced, it contained butterscotch caramel, cherry cream, fudge, orange jelly, nougat, coconut, and butter cream topped with chocolate.

Trudeau's records from the thirties show that it had first use of the trademark Seven Up, despite the efforts of the 7 Up Bottling Company to claim first use. To settle the dispute, Pearson sold the name to the 7 Up Bottling Company, which then leased the trademark back to Pearson on a long-term basis.

When the Pearson Candy Company became a part of a larger group of confectioners based in the Midwest, the 7 Up Bottling Company repurchased the license agreement, with the right to manufacture the product. It looks as if the Seven Up bar will probably not appear again.

Give a Yodel

The Nestlé Company, Inc., is a subsidiary of the parent Nestlé organization in Switzerland. The company makes a number of chocolate products, some of which are candy bars.

The Nestlé Milk Chocolate Bar was introduced in the United States in 1919. Today, the bar is nationally distributed in several sizes. When it was introduced, the bar quickly became a favorite of chocolate lovers, who preferred this distinctively creamy smooth milk chocolate bar. The Nestlé Chocolate Bar with Almonds was also introduced in 1919.

The Nestlé Crunch bar was introduced in 1938. Crisped rice, mixed with milk chocolate, made for a delicious, crunchy bar. The name Crunch describes precisely the sound made as one chews a bite of this nifty bar.

In the 1930s a cartoon series, "Nestlé's Nest," appeared on the Sunday comic pages. Both five-cent Nestlé Milk

Chocolate and Nestlé Milk Chocolate Bar with Almonds were featured in the ads. In the early fifties the cartoon character Neddy Nestlé appeared in a series of adventures featuring Nestlé Crunch bars.

In the late 1950s, the hottest programs on TV were quiz shows like "The $64,000 Question," "The $64,000 Challenge," "Twenty-One," and "The Big Surprise." The last show of "The Big Surprise" was in 1957, when Mike Wallace was the emcee. On this quiz program, the contestant chose a subject area and was then asked to answer ten questions, ranging in value from $100 to $100,000. The program sparked the idea for a new Nestlé product, introduced in 1966, the Nestlé $100,000 Bar, whose name suggests its top-price qualities. The bar combined chewy caramel with crisped rice enrobed in milk chocolate. The Nestlé $100,000 Bar captured the public's fancy when it was introduced, and it's still popular today (though $100,000 doesn't mean as much as it did way back in 1966).

Several years ago the Nestlé parent organization had tremendous success in Switzerland, Canada, and Argentina with an aerated bar. An aerated bar is made of whipped chocolate, which has a light consistency when it hardens.

In 1971, the Choco'Lite bar was introduced and manufactured in the United States. The bar, of whipped milk chocolate containing crispy honey-flavored chips, was the first aerated bar ever manufactured in the United States. Choco'Lite is recognizable by its brown wrapper with bold yellow lettering. The regular bar in early 1981 weighed 1 ounce; the king size, 5 ounces; and miniatures, .27 ounce each. Choco'Lite rapidly became a favorite, and for some unknown reason is especially popular with the junior high school crowd.

A new Nestlé product, the Go Ahead bar, first came out in 1981. The Go Ahead is a crunchy peanut-butter bar in milk chocolate, and is fortified with vitamins. Another new Nestlé item is the Animals Bar.

The Nestlé Company prides itself on producing a rich creamy chocolate that has both a smooth texture and a lustrous shine. Who knows what new bars will emerge from the Nestlé kitchens in years to come?

From Chewing Gum to a Delightful Mouthful

William A. Goetze started the Baltimore Chewing Gum Company in 1895. Goetze was one of the pioneers in the chewing gum business, and may have been the first to produce bubble gum. By 1915, a caramel product called Chu-ees was being manufactured in the Goetze factory. Chu-ees were packaged and wrapped in a fashion similar to chewing gum.

Then, in 1918, a great thing happened. The first Goetze's Caramel Creams came off the production line. The name explains exactly what the product was (and still is): a caramel jacket with a pure sugar cream center. Goetze's Caramel Creams really caught on, and the gum-making part of the business was gradually phased out. In 1950, the name of the company was changed to Goetze's Candy Company.

Caramel Creams come in five flavors — vanilla, licorice, chocolate, strawberry, and peanut butter — and are packaged in numerous ways. If you're a caramel lover and have never tried Goetze's Caramel Creams, you have a taste treat in store for you.

Chew, Chew, Chew That Candy Bar

What contains peanuts, sugar, corn syrup, molasses, chocolate, dextrose, and salt? Peanut Chews, made by the Goldenberg Candy Company of Philadelphia. Primarily a regional product, Peanut Chews are marketed mostly in the Eastern states.

The Goldenberg Candy Company was founded in 1890. A product called Walnut Loaf was developed, and from it evolved the formula for Peanut Chews. It appeared as a bulk confection shortly after the turn of the century. Goldenberg is a family-owned company that today manufactures only two products: Peanut Chews and Chew-ets. Peanut Chews were a popular penny-candy item in the East for years. The bar made its appearance in 1920, and has been going strong ever since. A companion product, Chew-ets, came on the scene in the 1930s. Chew-ets are a milk chocolate–coated version of Peanut Chews.

Heidi? No, Heide

Heidi was a Swiss girl in a novel by Johanna Spyri. Henry Heide was a German immigrant who got started in the candy business by selling boxes of candy door to door in New York City.

In 1869, Heide decided to produce his own candies. Working in a small cellar room in the big city, he produced popular counter candies, such as coconut cakes, peppermint sticks, and molasses lumps.

Heide's first big order was for 200 boxes of molasses lumps. The wagon was almost loaded with the boxes when something happened. The blind horse drawing the delivery wagon decided to investigate where the delicious molasses smell was coming from. The blind horse, wagon, and 200 boxes of molasses lumps went tumbling and crashing down the basement stairs. The horse (not hurt by the tumble) and wagon had to be extricated by the fire department. No one really knows for sure whether or not that first order was finally delivered.

Henry Heide was not to be outdone by the antics of a horse. His reputation as a candy maker grew rapidly. Many famous boxed candies and candy bars were introduced over the years. By 1962, a modern plant in New Brunswick, New Jersey, was erected and is still the home of the company.

Heide products bring back pleasant memories of carefree childhood days when boxes of Licorice Pastilles and Glycerine Gums were consumed in wild abandon. Some other childhood favorites were Jujubes, Jujyfruits, Red Hot Dollars, and Mexican Hats.

Jujubes were first produced some time before 1920. The jujube is an edible berry that grows in tropical climes. But the name of the berry has nothing to do with the make-up of the candy, which is more likely related to one of the basic ingredients of both Jujubes and Jujyfruits, ju-ju gum. (A jujube tree, by the way, was planted in front of the Heide plant several years ago, and has flourished despite some rather rigorous winters in New Jersey.)

Jujyfruits first appeared on the market in 1920. Each box contained an assortment of fruit-shaped and fruit-flavored candy pieces.

Red Hot Dollars were introduced in either 1925 or 1926; they were round pieces of gum candy bearing the dollar sign imprint. The "red hot" referred to a popular slang expression of the times; something that was new, up to date, and very popular was considered red hot. The name had nothing to do with the flavor, which was (and still is) raspberry.

Mexican Hats were also introduced in either 1925 or 1926. At first, the product was called Wetem and Wearem. Wetem and Wearem were hat-shaped pieces that were intended to be wetted by children and then affixed to the forehead. The name was changed to Mexican Hats in the 1930s, when the candy was packed in bulk.

Some other well-known Heide boxed products are Chocolate Babies, Diamond Licorice Drops, and such new items as Cap'n Melon, Cap'n Hot, Cap'n Punch, and Cap'n Cherry.

Before moving to New Jersey, Heide also made a number of candy bars: Coconut Bon Bons, Peanut Clusters, Brazil Nut, Chocolate Dates, Chocolate Cream Cakes, Chocolate Peppermint, Italian Chocolate, and Jumbo Chocolate Marshmallow Bar (introduced in 1924). Chocolate Sponge, which was first produced by Greenfields in 1901, was acquired by Heide in 1937, and later sold to the Schutter Candy Company.

Nonchocolate items, such as Peppermint Cream Wafer Rolls and Wintergreen Cream Wafer Rolls, were also produced, as well as Jelettes, first made in 1900.

A candy bar called Buck Private was introduced in 1943 and produced until early 1946. It was composed of chocolate and peanuts and was a fast-selling item during the war years. Heide produced Buck Private in the Eastern

United States, and another candy manufacturing company produced the bar in the West.

When Henry Heide, Inc., moved to the new factory in 1962, all chocolate bar items and hard candy items were eliminated. Heide continues to manufacture its best-known products, however, and may Jujyfruits, Jujubes, Red Hot Dollars, and Mexican Hats continue to roll off the production line forevermore!

And All Because of a Malfunctioning Machine

Cornelius Crane was the head of a plumbing fixture empire. Irving Crane was a famous billiard player, and Ichabod Crane was the headless horseman chronicled by Washington Irving. But who was Clarence A. Crane? His name won't mean much, but the product he manufactured will.

Clarence A. Crane was a small manufacturer of chocolate candies in Cleveland, Ohio, in 1912. Because chocolate sales dropped off in warm weather, Crane developed a summertime line of hard mints. Since Crane didn't have the space or the equipment in his factory, he used a pill manufacturer to press the mints into shape. The pill manufacturer, whose machine was malfunctioning, found that the pressing process worked much better when the hard mints were stamped out with a hole in the middle. Crane, taking a quick look at this distinctive candy shape, said, "Aha! I'll just call my new mint candies Crane's Life Savers!" Then Edward J. Noble, an advertising salesman, entered the scene. Noble bought the formula for Life Savers from Crane for $2900 in 1913. The mints became officially known as Pep-O-Mint Life Savers.

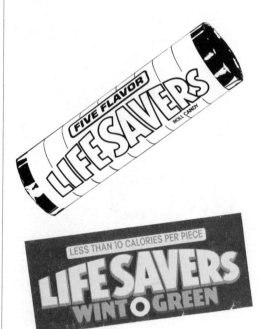

Noble ran into trouble immediately. He was unaware that in about a week's time the mints became stale and flavorless. The product's old-fashioned cardboard packaging absorbed the peppermint flavor, and all zip and zing was lost. Noble devised a tin-foil wrapping to seal in the mint flavor, but retailers wouldn't accept the foil-wrapped mints when they still had stale paper-wrapped mints on hand.

So began an elaborate sales pitch. Noble began canvassing saloons, cigar stores, drug stores, barber shops, and restaurants. He had the candy placed, with a five-cents price card on it, near the cash register. He then requested that the cashier make sure that each customer, regardless of what he or she bought, got a nickel in the change being returned. A nickel in the hand meant the sale of a pack of Life Savers. The idea moved like wildfire, and one of the biggest chain stores of the time, United Cigar Stores, bought the idea for their own use. Noble's fortune was on its way.

Noble took out his first advertisement in a 1918 issue of *The Saturday Evening Post*. In that year Life Savers were known as "the candy mint on everyone's tongue."

The first Pep-O-Mint Life Savers rolls were packaged by hand by girls who speared mints on a fork, then laid them on a sheet of tin foil held in a wooden fixture. In 1919, machinery was developed to assemble the mints automatically. And in 1925, aluminum foil, just newly perfected, took the place of the less bright and attractive tin foil.

In 1920, five flavors of Life Savers were available in single-flavor rolls of pressed mints. In 1924, rolls of boiled

←If she's always "busy" like this . . .

(when you and she should be like this)➡

←TRY THIS

➡ EVERYBODY'S BREATH offends sometimes after eating, drinking, or smoking. Let LIFE SAVERS save yours.

PEP·O·MINT LIFE SAVERS

Choice of 11 delicious mint and fruit flavors. Sold everywhere. 5

If she acts "all bored" like this . . .

When you'd rather be "all aboard" like this . . .

HONEYMOON EXP

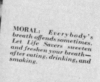

TRY THIS

MORAL: Everybody's breath offends sometimes. Let Life Savers sweeten and freshen your breath—after eating, drinking, and smoking.

WINT O GREEN LIFE SAVERS

Only 5¢

Delicious flavor change
Butter-Rum

...still only 5¢

Good luck
good lick !

...Still only 5¢

drops in lemon, lime, orange, and assorted flavors went on the market. The boiled drops were solid discs, until production technology reached the stage where the hole, already made famous by Life Savers mints, could be made in the drops.

The Wint-O-Green mint has an interesting story all of its own. Wint-O-Green, when chewed in the dark, is said to throw off sparks. The phenomenon, scientifically known as triboluminescence, occurs because of the rapid breaking of sugar crystals and the effect of the released energy on the flavoring. It's a challenge to kids at a party to see who can chomp out the most sparks in a darkened room!

Beech-Nut hard roll candy (various flavors) was the principal competitor of Life Savers before World War II. Beech-Nut ceased hard roll candy production during the war and concentrated on the chewing gum line it had already established.

Both Life Savers and Beech-Nut confectionery products were part of the Squibb Corporation for a number of years, and now are owned by Nabisco Brands, Inc.

In the sixty-eight years that Life Savers have existed, about 30 billion rolls have been produced (340 billion individual candies). Those 30 billion rolls, if stacked end to end, would create a delicious candy tunnel crossing the United States from coast to coast 280 times!

Mary, Mary, Quite Contrary, Au Contraire!

Mary Jane is sixty-eight years old and still going strong. This candy is continually finding new friends among younger generations, and also providing adults with remembrances of their youth, when they ate such beloved penny candies as Mary Janes.

In 1914, the Charles N. Miller Company began manufacturing Mary Janes. Mr. Miller named the candy after a favorite aunt. Over the years the company has tried out variations on the basic molasses and peanut-butter flavor, but no new products measured up to the criteria established by the original Mary Jane. Unable to come up with anything as good as their original product, the Miller Company produces just a single candy, Mary Jane, in several formats. Individually wrapped squares are bagged in 5-, 7- 8¾-, and 10½-ounce bags. They are available in all areas of the country except for the Western states. But the Miller Company plans to enter that market soon.

There's also a Mary Jane candy bar. It sells principally in New York City, though limited quantities are sold in New England. When first introduced in the 1950s, the Mary Jane Bar sold for a nickel; later for a dime; on to fifteen cents; and now for around twenty-five cents. Minor changes in weight accompanied the price changes. The Mary Jane Bars are scored, so a customer can break them into bite-size pieces.

Those of us in the Mary Jane Fan Club wish the star well and hope we can be around to celebrate her hundredth birthday in 2014!

The First American Candy Machine

In 1847 Oliver Chase invented the first American candy machine, a lozenge cutter, and began to manufacture Chase Lozenges. The original lozenge was diamond-shaped; Chase's lozenges, however, were round.

Chase first made his lozenges by hand. He used a funnel-like tube to cut out lozenge discs from a "paste" rolled out in sheets. The machine he developed looked like a clothes wringer with a series of holes cut in the roller. A sheet of the candy paste was fed into one side of the machine, and the cut pieces emerged as the rollers were turned. The machine was patented in 1847.

That year, Oliver and his brother founded Chase and Company. Their lozenge products were the forerunners of the present-day favorites manufactured by the New England Confectionery Company of Cambridge, Massachusetts — NECCO Wafers, and Canada Mints, Wintergreen, and Spearmint Lozenges.

The New England Confectionery Company was formed in 1901, when two other pioneers of the candy business in the Boston area joined forces with the Chase Company. Daniel Fobes was one of the partners. He began his business in 1848 and created new confections from such natural products as popcorn and maple sugar. The third partner,

William Wright, was instrumental in the growth of the Wright and Monk Company. Its trademark, O.K., was found on many of the popular penny items of that day. There was even an O.K. bar produced by NECCO, but it's no longer in existence.

The three partners joined forces to produce a complete general line of confectionery products under a new trademark, NECCO, patented in 1901 and derived from the initials of the new company.

Canada Mints first appeared in the Canadian market during the late 1880s and found an appreciative audience in the United States in 1908. NECCO Wafers, as a brand name, was introduced in 1912, but had been previously manufactured as Peerless Wafers. NECCO Wafers were recognized as quick sources of energy by hardy explorers like Donald MacMillan and Richard Byrd, who took them along on trips to the Arctic and South Pole respectively. Byrd took along two and a half tons.

Several successful candy bars are also manufactured by NECCO. Sky Bar was introduced in 1937 and was the first molded chocolate bar with four distinctly different centers. Every bar consists of four milk chocolate–enrobed sections each with an interior of caramel, vanilla, peanut, or fudge. Sky Bar was first announced to the public by means of a sky-writing campaign. That proved to be rather a dramatic way to present a new candy bar in the 1930s.

Bolster, a peanut crunch bar covered with milk chocolate, was put on the market in 1930. In the 1940s, a cartoon called "The Bolsters," about a family of that name, appeared on the comic pages of many Sunday newspapers. The Bolster bar was featured in those adventure ads.

NECCO Peanut Crunch, another crunchy peanut product coated with chocolate, was launched in 1977. Caramel is featured in NECCO Milk Chocolate Caramel Roll, a 1974 introduction, and peppermint in NECCO Chocolate Twin Mint Patties. The latter item appeared under that name in 1954, but had originally been known as Wilson's Chocolate Mint.

During its 135-year existence, NECCO has played its part in the American way of life. Almost every child today can identify a roll of NECCO Wafers, and the mere mention of the name brings from adults fond reminiscences of childhood.

Does the Ding A Lings candy bar ring a bell? The Ding A Lings bar (crisped rice, caramel, peanut-butter wafer, and chocolate) is approximately ten years old, and comes out of the F&F Laboratories, Inc., of Chicago, a cough drop and confections manufacturer.

Started in 1928 by Morris Fox in Omaha, Nebraska, the company moved to Illinois in 1936. Sherbits candy rolls were added to the Ding A Lings bars in 1946. A line of candy bars and other candy products are now being manufactured under the Foxes label. One Foxes bar product is a natural yogurt bar and is called just that, Yogurt. Some other Foxes bar products are Peanut Butter Wafers, Creme Sugar Wafers, and Nutty Logs. An F&F Daily-C candy roll is also produced; there are 250 milligrams of vitamin C in every tablet.

Although not strictly within the bounds of this book, two F&F products are of interest because of the niche they occupy as Americana products, Sen-Sen and Smith Brothers Cough Drops.

Sen-Sen, acquired by F&F in 1977, had its heyday in the 1930s. It was a confection that became widely known as a breath freshener. It came (and still does) in rectangular pellet form in small packets. The product's name was so well known in the 1930s that people had it on their tongues both physically and literally. In keeping with the times, a Sen-Sen sugarless mint was introduced in 1980.

When Sen-Sen was owned by the American Chicle Company in the 1950s, numerous radio commercials were produced for Sen-Sen. One of the sixty-second radio commercials broadcast over a New York City station in 1957 went like this:

(Gong)
ANNOUNCER (in Chinese manner):
Is well-known fact — dragons very unpopular . . . because dragons have very bad breath.
(Growl . . . Whoosh)
Is also well known — people with dragon breath unpopular, too — possible candidates for very single life. Please

to hear helpful words regarding dragon breath from Cho Cho Sen-Sen. (*Gong*)

GIRL (in Chinese manner):

Old Chinese proverb say: Bad breath death of romance. But Sen-Sen give you *breath* of romance. (*Gong*) Sen-Sen is tiny, tiny, tasty, tasty square you can pop in your mouth anywhere. Very exotic flavor — like tropical flower. Romantic scent — very exciting, very inviting. Yet just one tiny Sen-Sen keep breath sweet an hour or more! Will not repeat what you eat . . . or drink . . . or smoke. Sen-Sen keep your secret. Keep you safe from bad dragon's breath.

ANNOUNCER (in Chinese manner):

Replace bad breath with breath of *romance*. Get Sen-Sen. (*Gong*)

GIRL (close to mike):

Breath scented with Sen-Sen very romantic!

F&F Laboratories acquired Smith Brothers Cough Drops in 1972. The two Smith Brothers shown on the package were affectionately known as Trade and Mark, but their real names were William and Andrew. (Andrew's picture was above the word *Mark*; William's was above the word *Trade*.) The two brothers helped found Smith Brothers in Poughkeepsie, New York, in 1817. Now 165 years old, Smith Brothers Cough Drops remain a leader in the cough drop field.

For a few years the F&F Laboratories instituted the Smith Brothers National Whiskers Association, which is no longer functioning. The rules for joining were: "Any bearded gentleman can join by sending in his name, address, and 25¢ in coin and a front panel, or a reasonable facsimile, from a box of Smith Brothers Cough Drops to F&F Laboratories, 221 N. LaSalle Street, Chicago, Illinois 60601. In return he will receive an 8 × 10″ certificate suitable for framing, attesting to membership in the Association. Honorary memberships are also available to distaff members."

So, in closing, if Trade and Mark don't clear up that tickle in your throat, or if Sen-Sen doesn't take your breath away, just pick up a Ding A Lings candy bar and gorge yourself.

On the Banks of the Wabash? No, the Mississippi

C. C. Washburn erected his first flour mill on the banks of the Mississippi River in 1866. The mill was built for the recently formed Washburn Crosby Company. Fourteen years later, the Washburn Crosby Company had the top flour entry in a Miller's International Exhibition. The gold medal awarded the flour resulted in the name Gold Medal being given to the product. The company, over the years, developed into the organization now known as General Mills, Inc.

General Mills began producing a line of granola products under the name Nature Valley Granola Bars in 1975. There were three flavors: Oats'n Honey, Cinnamon, and Coconut. In 1977 Peanut was introduced; in 1979, Roasted Almonds.

Also marketed are Nature Valley Granola Clusters. National distribution began in 1980. Clusters are available in three flavors: Caramel, Almond, and Raisin. A recent introduction is the Nature Valley Crisp bar. It contains rice and honey, peanut butter, and cinnamon.

Both Nature Valley Granola Bars and Granola Clusters contain grain products, and so bring a new dimension to the bar business. They are sweet-tooth satisfiers of the first order.

And Bingo Was His Name

Besides Buster Brown's dog, Tige, who are three well-known fictional dogs in America? One of them is the dog who appeared beside a gramophone, for RCA, along with the words "His Master's Voice." That dog's name? Nipper.

The second dog, Lassie, was featured in *Lassie Come Home*, written by Eric Knight in 1940. This book became a real favorite with kids, and led to Lassie's appearance as a TV star in the 1950s and 1960s. Although Lassie was a female, on TV she was always played by a male dog!

Another widely recognized dog is Bingo, the likable mutt who poses with the Sailor Boy on packages of Cracker Jack.

Little did Frederick William Rueckheim, a German immigrant, know what was in store for him when he came to Chicago after the Great Fire of 1871. Rueckheim first opened a popcorn stand, but by 1885 he had a factory.

Right in the middle of Chicago's first World's Fair, the Columbian Exposition of 1893, Rueckheim sold his new popcorn-peanuts-and-molasses confection. But the product didn't have a name until 1896, when a salesman, munching on a handful, said, "That's a cracker jack!" F. W. Rueckheim quickly latched on to the last two words and christened his product with them. In the same year, 1896, a customer thought up a slogan that helped sell millions of boxes of Cracker Jack at five cents each. That famous slogan was "The More You Eat the More You Want."

Cracker Jack was sold in baseball parks starting early in the 1900s. Popular as a ball park snack, it was consequently immortalized in 1908, when Jack Norworth wrote the lyrics for "Take Me Out to the Ball Game." The line from that song that everyone remembers is "Buy me some peanuts and Cracker Jack."

In 1910 and 1911, coupons printed on Cracker Jack boxes could be redeemed for prizes. In 1912 the coupons were discontinued, and prizes were packed inside the Cracker Jack boxes. The sales then became really dramatic.

The Sailor Boy and his dog, Bingo, weren't added as the national logo for Cracker Jack until the outbreak of World

War I. The Sailor Boy was modeled after Rueckheim's grandson Robert, but was named Jack. There was a child's song about a pet dog around at the time that contained the line ". . . and Bingo was his name," and this may have been the source of the dog's name. Over the last seventy years, Jack and Bingo have been modified only slightly.

In 1932–1934, the Mystery, or Question Mark, package was introduced. More than 230,000 kids joined the Mystery Club. They received toys as prizes in return for coins and the cards packaged in the Mystery and Question Mark boxes.

New products (none of them successful) were introduced in the Depression years by the manufacturers of Cracker Jack. Twister Bars, Zulu Bars, New Wrinkle, and Mallow Whip and Cream are all memories now, but Cracker Jack persists as a favorite of Americans.

Many nostalgia buffs now make a hobby of collecting the toy prizes that were offered in the packages from 1912 on. The owner of the original collection of prizes, of course, is Cracker Jack, in Chicago. A bank vault in the plant contains more than 10,000 rare prizes. Not all the prizes have been stored away, however; some of them are showcased in a glass display in the headquarters' lobby.

More than sixteen billion toys have been given out since 1912, all inserted in Cracker Jack boxes by hand. The toy insertion process hasn't yet been automated. More than 500 different toys are inserted in boxes each day. In 1980, Cracker Jack launched a Super Toy Surprise Campaign. In that year 57,000 boxes holding Super Prizes were scattered among the 400 million boxes of Cracker Jack lining store shelves. The Super Prizes were coupons entitling lucky holders to such freebees as Mazda station wagons (to entice adult buyers), Mattel games, tricycles, and Barbie dolls.

And now for a final bit of Cracker Jack nostalgia. Back in the pre–Jack and Bingo Cracker Jack days, you could "Send name and address with 2¢ stamp and receive a full set (20 different kinds) of our famous 'Cracker Jack' Riddle cards."

A few of the chestnuts that were hot numbers back in the early part of the century were:

What is worse than raining dogs or cats?
Hailing omnibusses.

What grows the less tired the more it works?
A carriage wheel.

Why is the Fourth of July like an oyster?
Because we cannot enjoy it without crackers.

And to close, it would be most appropriate to use an advertising jingle of those early Cracker Jack years —

It is not often one can find
A candy good for body and mind,
But our old doctor says it's true
That "Cracker Jack" is good for you.

Banned in Boston? Heck No

Back in the 1920s, almost all confectionery houses made a general line of candies — hard, soft, caramels, chocolates, bars, you name it. Most of them were distributed regionally; only a few confectioners distributed on a national basis. In the Los Angeles area, for example, there were approximately twenty-five candy manufacturers, each making a variety of products, including candy bars. The candy bars were, for the most part, labeled and identified descriptively if trade names weren't used. Such descriptive labels as Milk Chocolate Bar, Brazil Nut Bar, and Cocoanut and Cherry Whip were preceded by the manufacturing company's name. That meant there was a bunch of Milk Chocolate Bars and Brazil Nut Bars available. Customers, consequently, acquired an attachment for a company name rather than a trademark, which is somewhat different from today, when the tendency is to identify the trademark, not the manufacturer. For example, almost everyone knows Baby Ruth, Reese's Peanut Butter Cups, Snickers, and the $100,000 Bar, but who knows they are owned by Nabisco Confections, Inc., Hershey, M&M/Mars, and the Nestlé Company respectively?

Though trademarks are the norm today, there are still some manufacturers around who package their bars in clear wrappers, with the bar's identity handwritten on a label attached to the head of the wrapper. One such firm is the venerable Bailey's, established in Boston in 1873. Bailey's candies are retailed in eight locations in the Greater Boston area (and are sold by mail order, too). Headquarters and the candy plant are located right in downtown Boston, in a narrow, four-story building, the ground floor of which serves as a retail store and ice cream parlor. Bailey's makes a few candy bars; some of its hand-labeled ones are Marshmallow Bar (1980), Fudge Bar (1977), and Bailey Bars, of milk, dark, or white chocolate (1971). The Ting-a-Ling Bar is a combination bar developed in 1969 when someone in the Bailey organization realized that lots of good scrap candy was being discarded from other candy products being made. The Ting-a-Ling is made of peanut-butter and molasses-chip scraps covered with milk chocolate.

The Pretzel Bar (1980) has pretzel remnants from chocolate-covered pretzels covered with milk, white, or dark chocolate. And the Holiday Hash Bar (1975) is made of crisped rice, walnuts, and colored marshmallows, coated in a white chocolate. The result is a real winner. Were Cotton Mather and others still around, they'd make sure that the Holiday Hash Bar would be banned in Boston, because it's sinfully good.

There's More Than Beer in Milwaukee

When I was a kid growing up in the Midwest in the 1930s, Milwaukee was noted for two things. It was the beer capital of the United States, and it had a great German restaurant, Mäders, where my folks would take me to eat on occasion.

Then, in 1945, a confectionery company, Chocolate House, came into being in Milwaukee. One of its acquisitions was the Maronn Candy Company, which first produced Whipped Creme Eggs in 1917. Whipped Creme Eggs are still being produced by the original formula. When it was introduced, this candy was made only for the Easter

market, but it's now manufactured all year long. Added in recent years to capture other seasonal markets are Whipped Creme Pumpkin, Whipped Creme Santa, and Whipped Creme Hearts. A Mint Whip is also being produced.

In 1961 Chocolate House pioneered the Frosted Pretzel, a salted pretzel with a white coating. Candy bars were first produced by them in 1960, and were sold at retail for fifteen cents when nickel bars were still around. The bars were popular, so the price differential apparently wasn't a sales problem.

Approximately half a dozen bars are now produced. Favorites are Meltaway, Mint Nut, Cream Caramel, and Chocolate Nut Fudge bars. Chocolate House candy bar products are now available in all fifty states.

Up in O-Hi-O

Arthur Garfield Spangler was a true entrepreneur. In 1906, he purchased the Gold Leaf Baking Powder Company, set up production in Bryan, Ohio, and went out on the baking powder sales circuit. Arthur picked up additional items to handle when his mother began salting peanuts in her home, and at the suggestion of brother Ernest, he took on candy as a wholesale line.

In 1911, the company ventured into making candy. The first product was the Spangler Cocoanut Ball. Preparing the coconut was a big challenge in those days. An arrangement was made with the Park Hotel, located next door, to allow steam from the hotel's steam bath to be piped into the factory. There, the coconuts were steamed while still in their boxes. Then they were cracked by workers using hatchets. The crackers earned $1.50 a day, considered good wages in 1911.

The Cocoanut Ball became extremely popular, and was sold in F. W. Woolworth and Kresge variety stores across the country. It was discontinued in 1924.

A line of chocolates was added in 1911. The Cream Peanut Cluster, still a popular item, was one of the first chocolate products.

Another early favorite was Cherry Ball. A maraschino cherry was deposited in a cream center. After the center

hardened, it was hand-pressed into an ice cream dipper that had previously been filled with ground peanuts and chocolate. The resulting goody was then placed on a tray with other Cherry Balls to cool before being hand-wrapped in foil.

In 1931, Spangler purchased the formula and trademark for chocolate-coated Hickok Honeycomb Chips. That candy had been invented accidentally in 1892, when taffy drippings, collected around the edges and outsides of the kettles, were sampled by an employee of the Hickok firm and found to be really tasty! The inventive employee then suggested that the chips be coated with chocolate. The resulting candy, with a mellow molasses flavor and honeycombed air holes, was a good seller for years. The candy was sold in bar form by Spangler as Hickok's Honeycomb Chocolate Chips, popular in the 1940s and fifties.

The Spangler Company produced a number of other candy bars in the forties and fifties. The golden Jitney Bar was a maple cream peanut cluster bar. There was also a vanilla-flavored Jitney Bar. A maple-flavored marshmallow and peanut bar, enrobed in chocolate, was the Maplette bar. Some other Spangler bars were Macaroon bar, Champion, Chester bar, and the Spangler bar, somewhat similar in nature to the Clark bar. Still others were Nut Loaf bar, Caramel bar, and maple-flavored Sugar Cake.

In 1953, Spangler purchased the trade name Dum Dum lollipops, originated in 1924. The ball-shaped candy on a stick was named for the dum-dum bullet used in World War I. An early sales manager of the Akron Candy Company said he remembered the bullets, and figured *dum-dum* was a word any child could say.

MAY 19 1955

DAVY CROCKETT

that red hot merchandising theme

HITS THE CANDY COUNTER

The name and story of one of America's great national heros is now the selling rage. Climb aboard that covered wagon! Summer is always the season for Western motif. Summer is likewise when lollipops and suckers sell in terrific volume.

DAVY CROCKETT BIG POPS

Giant oversize-suckers that add Color and Sales to your candy section. The famous A-Z Big Suckers are no_ Davy Crockett design.

Each 6 inch circular pop is on a beautiful foot tall sucker. A ch 10 assorted flavors and the 10 pops are packed in the uniqu

built-in counter display. Three different colors of pops are assor shipping case. Gross case weight is 40 lbs.

The regular A-Z Big Suckers are of course available. You can mix

DAVY CROCKETT

BIG POP

INGR: SUGAR, CORN SYRUP, ART FLAVOR CERT. USP COLORING NET WT. 6 OZ.

SPANGLER CANDY CO.   BRYAN, OHIO

RUSH RUSH RUSH:

Cases	Boxes	Item			
		Davy Crockett Big Pop	12 ct. display bx.	6 bxs. to cs.	1.70 dz. f.o.b.
	29¢	A-Z Big Suckers	12 ct. display bx.	6 bxs. to cs.	1.65 dz. f.o.b.

We Ship
The Day
Order Is
Received!

➡

ORDER NOW

BIG SUCKERS
SPANGLER CANDY CO. BRYAN, OHIO
BIG SUCKERS

90

In 1955, Davy Crockett became a national craze. His name was plastered everywhere, and fans of the TV "Disneyland" show about his exploits were legion. The Spangler Company developed a special sucker called Davy Crockett Big Pop. Crockett's face was on a paper insert beneath the polyethylene overwrap. (The sucker without the Crockett insert was sold as the A-Z Big Sucker.)

Pressed tablet candy and hard candy rolls were added in 1965 — Kraks and Smiles. In 1978, Lite-Mint Rolls were introduced. And in 1978, the Saf-T-Pop trade name was purchased from the Curtiss Candy Division of Standard Brands. The Saf-T-Pop featured a patented, looped fiber-cord handle. It's the only lollipop in the nation that is individually wrapped, handle and all. In 1980, All Natural Pops, in four flavors, came off the production line.

Were Arthur Garfield Spangler around today, he'd be spanking proud of what's emerged from his modest beginnings as a baking powder manufacturer. When it comes to candy specialty products, Spangler's banner is star-spangled.

The Year the First Income Tax Was Levied

In 1861, the first United States income tax was levied to raise money for the Union Army and Navy. In that same year, William Schrafft, a Bavarian-American, opened a small store in Boston. Patrons of his store bought his gumdrops to send to Union soldiers in the field during the Civil War.

Success with his gumdrop sales enabled Schrafft to expand his business. It built up over the years until it became one of the largest confectionery producers in the United States.

Schrafft's manufactured a number of candy bars, and in the days when five-cent candy bars were sold, salesmen's cases displayed the various bar items. The bars looked real, the wrappers were real, but the insides were just made of padding of one kind or another, since real bars would

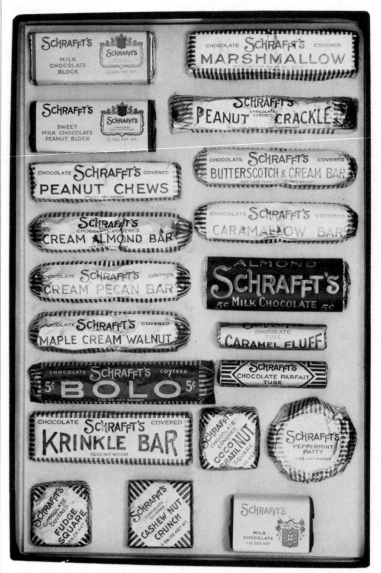

eventually have spoiled or melted. Among the bars displayed were Milk Chocolate Block, Milk Peanut Block, Peanut Chew, Cream Almond Bar, Cream Pecan Bar, Maple Cream Walnut, Krinkle Bar, Fudge Square, Cashew Nut Crunch, Coco-Brazil Nut Square, Peppermint Patty, Chocolate Parfait Tube, Caramel Fluff, Milk Chocolate Bar, Caramallow Bar, Butterscotch & Cream Bar, Peanut Crackle, and Marshmallow Bar.

Generally, the bars in a salesman's display case had descriptive, rather than trade, names. An exception in the Schrafft's display case was the Bolo Bar. That bar sold for five cents and was a combination of caramel, peanuts, and fudge, coated with milk chocolate.

The E. P. Lewis Company became a subsidiary of the Schrafft Company in later years. Originally located in Boston, the Lewis Company set up shop in Malden, Massa-

chusetts, in 1933. During the 1930s, 1940s, and 1950s, it produced a number of candy bars such as Lewis Peppermint (similar to Mason Mint), Lewis Nougat Bar, and Lewis Rainbow Jellies (similar to Chuckles). One of the Lewis products launched from the Schrafft factory in Sullivan Square in Charlestown, Massachusetts, was the 10:30 bar, advertised as "the candy that's something else." The 10:30 bar was made of crisped rice and a candied mixture that was covered with an off-white milk chocolate. It was a tasty bar and could be viewed through a clear wrapper, a sales enhancer, given the bar's appetizing appearance.

The Schrafft Company prospered over the years, but eventually fell on hard times. In 1981, it went out of business briefly before being taken over by new management, and now is producing a general line of candy.

A Winner at the $2 Window

William Loft and his wife first began making candies in their kitchen before opening a retail shop in New York City in 1860. That one store was the beginning of what was to become one of the largest candy store chains in the United States, until its decline.

In its heyday, Loft's made more than 350 different candies, specializing in individual pieces and boxed candies. Bar candies were not a major line, but Loft's became rather well known for its Parlay bar. That bar received its name from the racing terminology for a triple winner.

What's Your Favorite Brand of Scotch?

What is your favorite brand of Scotch? Cutty Sark? J&B? Chivas Regal? Mine is butterscotch. And no one makes a better one than Reed.

The Reed Candy Company, founded in Chicago in 1893, specializes in hard candies. Its most famous product, Reed's Butterscotch candy roll, was first manufactured in 1931. Before that, a round butterscotch wafer was manufactured. Several other flavors of candy rolls are now also manufactured by Reed.

The original safety-handle sucker, Paloops, was introduced by Reed in 1933. Packaged in a variety of ways, and in many flavors, Paloops have been a favorite of young kids for years.

In Their Cups

In Altoona, Pennsylvania, is a confectionery company, Boyer Bros., Inc., that manufactures cups — actually cup candies. Cup candies consist of various soft centers and coatings molded directly into crinkled glassine paper cups. Founded in 1936, Boyer Bros., Inc., specializes in producing candy bar items that come in cup form. One of their best-selling bars is Mallo Cup, milk chocolate coating containing coconut, with a whipped marshmallow cream center. Another cup, Fluffernutter, is a combination of marshmallow and peanut butter, covered with milk chocolate. Peanut Butter Cup has a peanut-butter center covered with milk chocolate. S'Mores combines graham cracker, marshmallow, and chocolate. Other Boyer cup bars are Bunch o' Nuts!, Milk 'n Cookies, Smoothie, and Minty Mallo. Smoothie has a center of peanut butter and

is coated with butterscotch. Minty Mallo has a mint-flavored marshmallow cream center covered with dark chocolate.

Without a doubt, Boyer bar cups runneth over with confectionery goodness. (Even though Fluffernutter, Bunch o' Nuts!, and Milk 'n Cookies are now deceased.)

Just off the Pennsylvania Turnpike

Deep in the heart of the Pennsylvania Dutch country can be found the Wilbur Chocolate Company. The Wilbur Company, located in Lititz, specializes in making chocolate for industrial users.

Originally located in Philadelphia, the Wilbur Company in 1894 began turning out a chocolate confection known as Wilbur Buds, which is still being produced.

In the 1930s and 1940s, the Wilbur Chocolate Company was a partnership called the Wilbur-Suchard Chocolate Company. The Swiss partner, Suchard, organized production, and the actual manufacturing was done by Wilbur Chocolate Company.

The Wilbur Company now produces a variety of chocolate bars: Wilbur Dark Sweet Chocolate, Wilbur Orange Milk Chocolate, Wilbur Peanut Butter Peanut, Wilbur Mint Chocolate Crunch, Wilbur Coffee Mint Chocolate, Wilbur White Almond Bark, Wilbur Milk Chocolate, Wilbur Milk Chocolate with Almonds, Wilbur Milk Chocolate Crunch, and Wilbur Chocolate Almond Toffee Crunch.

At the Wilbur factory in Lititz, a Candy Americana Museum was established in 1971. The museum is dedicated to candy memorabilia and displays an animated 1900 candy kitchen, as well as an actual candy kitchen in which handmade chocolates are produced.

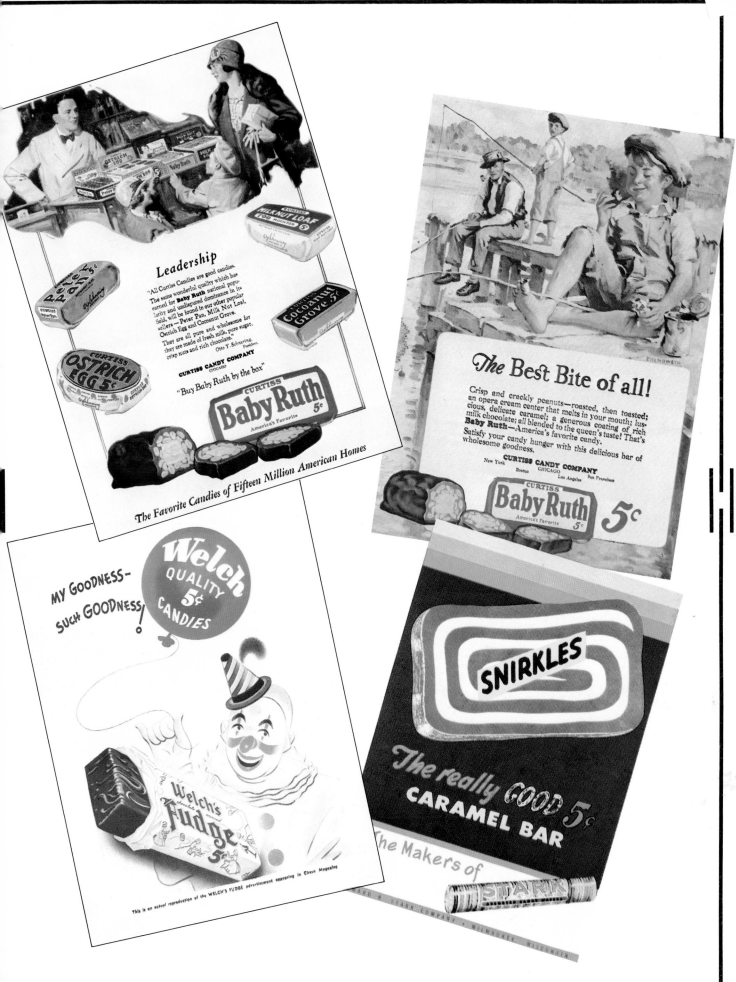

Early Candy Bar Advertisements

Candy Bar Wrappers of the 1940's

Contemporary Candy Bar Wrappers

Advertisements of the 1940's

Advertisement from The Saturday Evening Post, October 18, 1947

You've Come a Long Way,
Bee Bee

Bit-O-Honey appeared in 1924, a product of the Schutter-Johnson Company in Chicago. (Walter Johnson, it may be recalled, later split with Schutter to form his own company, and produced PowerHouse and other candy bar items now manufactured by Peter Paul Cadbury, Inc.)

Bit-O-Honey was a new kind of bar; it consisted of six pieces of candy wrapped in waxed paper and then packaged in a wrapper. Almond bits embedded in a honey-flavored taffy made for a long-chewing candy. The current bar wrapper displays an anthropomorphized bee smacking its lips, and carries the slogan, "Chews and chews and chews. If you're in a hurry . . . forget it!"

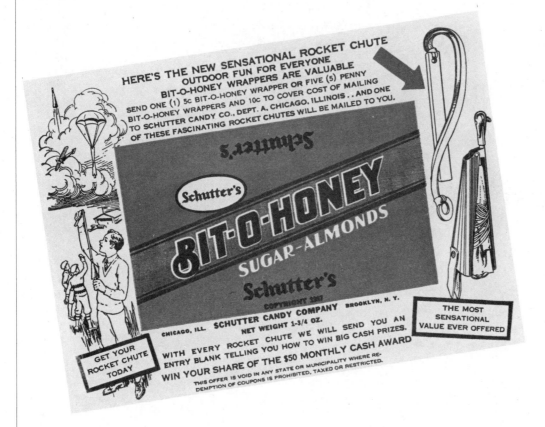

Some other Schutter bars were Golden Harvest, a bar containing walnuts, and Bit-O-Coconut, a bar that didn't sell too well. By the early 1960s the Schutter Company was sold to the Chunky Corporation in New York. Thus, all the Schutter bars, including Bit-O-Honey and another old-timer, Old Nick, had a new home. Old Nick was a nut roll bar similar to Baby Ruth and Oh Henry!

The Chunky Corporation, already owners of Oh Henry!, decided to retire the Old Nick label. Oh Henry! was popular throughout the country and so had more clout than Old Nick, which sold well only in the Midwest and in New England. The Old Nick label was temporarily put on hold, and when a New England confectioner looked into buying the name a few years later, he found that the brand had been off the market long enough to lose its recognition power. So Old Nick was never revived — it just languished away in the old trademark section of Candyland Cemetery.

Even though Old Nick is no longer with us, Bit-O-Honey (now manufactured by the Ward-Johnston Division of The Terson Company) is still going strong, almost sixty years after it first appeared. It's a long-lasting bar in more ways than one.

Handy Henry

The application for the trademark Oh Henry! was filed with the United States Patent Office in July of 1921 by the Williamson Candy Company of Chicago. The application stated the trademark had been in use since November 1920.

Contrary to what some people may believe, the Oh Henry! bar wasn't named after the author William Sydney Porter, who used the pseudonym "O. Henry" when he began writing short stories.

According to company records, here's how the bar *was* named. Mr. Williamson was operating a combination retail and wholesale candy store, and every day at about the same time, a young fellow named Henry would come into the store to talk and kid around with the girls who were making candy. Before long, the girls got into the habit of asking Henry to do little odd jobs and favors for them. They looked forward to his coming each day, and as soon as he'd come into the store you'd hear, "Oh, Henry, will you get me this?" Or, "Oh, Henry, will you get me that?"

Later in the year, when it came time to find a name for the nut roll that was being manufactured, Mr. Williamson's salesmen said, "All we hear around here is 'Oh, Henry,' so why not call the candy bar Oh Henry!"

Other bar products that were made a little later on by the Williamson Company were Choc-O-Nuts, Salted Nut Roll, and the Amos & Andy Bar, which was a good seller in the 1930s.

Oh Henry! has broken that old, old tradition . . the belief that fine candies come only in fine boxes.

For America's women have discovered that under Oh Henry!'s simple, homely garb lies a truly fine candy . . a "personal portion" that brings a new convenience into the eating of fine candy . . . and a luscious, lingering, nut-accented taste that marks Oh Henry! one of the finer things of life!

See for yourself . . in the bar . . or sliced!

Oh Henry! was one of the first bars to be launched nationally. The Williamson Company sent twenty-five salesmen to Los Angeles, as an example, to blanket the area with Oh Henry! promotion. The advertising blitz paid off, and Oh Henry! quickly became a national favorite. Now manufactured by the Ward-Johnston Division of The Terson Company, Oh Henry! is still called for around the country.

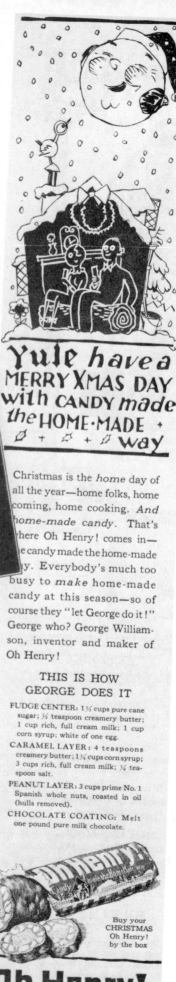

Yule have a MERRY XMAS DAY with candy made the HOME·MADE · way

Christmas is the *home* day of all the year—home folks, home coming, home cooking. *And home-made candy.* That's where Oh Henry! comes in— the candy made the home-made way. Everybody's much too busy to *make* home-made candy at this season—so of course they "let George do it!" George who? George Williamson, inventor and maker of Oh Henry!

THIS IS HOW GEORGE DOES IT

FUDGE CENTER: 1¾ cups pure cane sugar; ½ teaspoon creamery butter; 1 cup rich, full cream milk; 1 cup corn syrup; white of one egg.

CARAMEL LAYER: 4 teaspoons creamery butter; 1¾ cups corn syrup; 3 cups rich, full cream milk; ¾ teaspoon salt.

PEANUT LAYER: 3 cups prime No. 1 Spanish whole nuts, roasted in oil (hulls removed).

CHOCOLATE COATING: Melt one pound pure milk chocolate.

Buy your CHRISTMAS Oh Henry! by the box

Oh Henry!

CANDY MADE THE HOME-MADE WAY

Don't Call Me Slim, Okay?

It contained Brazil nuts, cashews, raisins, and chocolate, and came in a thick, almost square shape (to be more exact, the shape was that of a truncated pyramid). What better name for such a bar than Chunky? Chunky first saw the light of day in the mid-1930s, when a New York City candy maker and wholesale confectioner, Philip Silverstein, manufactured it. Silverstein named the candy after his granddaughter, who at that time was a "chunky" baby. Another of the company's bars was the Unique bar.

The original Chunky is still around, now being manufactured by the Ward-Johnston Division of The Terson Company. A Pecan Chunky and a Milk Chocolate Chunky are also now being made. Triple Chunky bars recently made their appearance, each bar containing three truncated pyramids, instead of just one.

The Goober Gang

Goober, a Southern word for peanut, made its way as a trademark for a product the Blumenthal Chocolate Company began manufacturing in 1925. The Blumenthal family had originated in North Carolina, and Goobers was a natural name to be picked by Southerners for the milk chocolate–covered peanuts they began to turn out.

The Blumenthal Chocolate Company, started in 1911 in the Philadelphia area, manufactured its first candy product in 1922. The product was Bob White, a large (2½ inches in diameter) nonpareil. In the late 1920s, the size of the Bob White was reduced drastically, to small, rounded wafers of chocolate covered with tiny pellets of sugar. These were marketed under the trade name Sno-Caps. In 1927, Raisinets, chocolate-covered raisins, first saw the light of day.

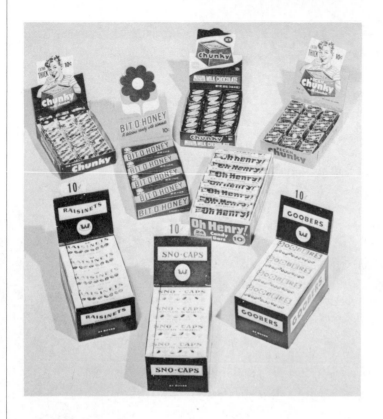

The Blumenthal Chocolate Company was acquired by Ward Foods in 1969, and in 1981 became a part of the Ward-Johnston Division of The Terson Company. Goobers, Raisinets, and Sno-Caps are special favorites among boxed-candy lovers, and are particularly popular with movie theater crowds.

Strolling Along the Avenue

William H. Luden incorporated the Luden's cough drop and confectionery company in 1881. It was located in a five-by-six-foot-space in the family home in Reading, Pennsylvania, where Father Luden's jewelry business was also carried on. Although he started as a candy manufacturer, William Luden was to make his fame as the developer of the menthol cough drop. Luden's cough drops, when introduced, weren't the traditional red color then associated with cough drops; they were amber. The public took a liking to them, and Luden's business was

off to the races. Some early promotion lines for Luden's cough drops were "Medicated for Clothespin Nose," "Medicated for Sandpaper Throat," and "Here's Relief from Smokestack Throat." (The last was directed to the smoking crowd.)

Luden's 5th Avenue bar was first produced in 1936. The bar, still very much alive, contains a crunchy peanut-butter center, two almonds, and is enrobed in milk chocolate. The name 5th Avenue conjures up an image of elegance and high style, an image of distinction, that even a candy bar manufacturer might want to capitalize on. To differentiate from the street of the same name, the numeral 5 was substituted for the word *fifth*, and the candy bar became 5th Avenue. Some other Luden bar and bar-related products are Mello Mint (1948), Rinkles (1952), and Super Nut (1952). (The Light Coated Marshmallow Santa Bar is a tasty Christmas item.)

The 5th Avenue bar, Luden's confectionery best seller, is still partly made by hand. After a batch of the peanut-butter center has been cooked and pulled out by machine, the batch is spread out on a marble table, where it is formed by hand. Put into another mixer, each bar then has two almonds placed on it before being enrobed in chocolate. 5th Avenue "tastes good, as a candy bar should!"

Long Live the Queen

A division of Luden's is the Queen Anne Candy Company, which first saw the light of day in Hammond, Indiana, in 1920. A number of candy bars have been manufactured by Queen Anne over the years: Pecan Meltaways, Mint Meltaways, Almond Rolls, Peanut Rolls, Cashew Rolls, Almond Treat, Queen High, and Queen Anne Nut Roll.

Among the first bars was the Queen Anne Pecan Roll, introduced in 1921. Made with a fudge center covered with caramel, and enrobed in pecans, the bar sold for ten cents in the 1940s. It was discontinued several years ago, but is still available as a family-size product.

Four delightful flavors blend in every bite!

First, freshly shelled, plump, royal pecans, a tender-crisp crust covering the whole top.

Then, the kind of caramel that can be made only with rich whole milk, and only in a way we spent years perfecting. *Next*, a center of real parfait fudge with *more* whole milk cooked in.

Last, a marvelous special-blend chocolate, smooth as whipping cream!

No skimping anywhere in this luxury treat! If the last bite—always just as wonderful as the first—seems to come too soon, remember next time to buy two!

More than candy—it's delicious food! *Enjoy it every day!*

Queen Anne Candy Company, Hammond, Ind.
Makers also of the 5c Queen Anne Almond Treat, another member of the Royal Family of Candy Bars

Queen Anne
PECAN ROLL

The Queen Anne Jingle Bar, with a fudge center covered with caramel, was topped with peanuts and enrobed in milk chocolate. It was introduced nationally in 1947 with an advertising promotion in the Sunday newspaper comic sections. The campaign featured $41,000 worth of prizes like Jeep station wagons, Moto-Scoots, movie cameras, bikes, and wrist watches. To be eligible for prize drawings, contestants had to write "last lines" to jingles printed on Queen Anne Jingle Bar wrappers. One typical wrapper jingle read,

> Jimmy got a Jingle Bar
> He loved each luscious bite
> Said he, "Queen Anne's Jingle Bar
>
> ——————————————————
>
> (you fill in)

At the present time Queen Anne puts out such goodies as Stocking Stuffer Milk Chocolate Marshmallow Santas and Snowmen, family-size Pecan and Cashew Logs, and, for the Easter season, Chocolate Marshmallow Eggs, Pecan Eggs, Chocolate Marshmallow Rabbits, Peanut Butter Eggs, and Assorted Cream Eggs.

Long live the Queen!

Amedeo Obici

Amedeo Obici came to America from Italy at the age of eleven. As a young adult he operated a peanut stand, which he expanded into a store and restaurant. Then, in partnership with his future brother-in-law, Mario Peruzzi, he started the Planters Nut and Chocolate Company, which was incorporated in 1906 in Wilkes-Barre, Pennsylvania. The company produced not only whole salted peanuts, but also chocolate-covered peanuts and chocolate nut bars.

In 1913, the company set up its own processing plant in Suffolk, Virginia, the heart of the peanut-producing country. Obici opened his own shelling plant so that he could buy directly from peanut farmers and eliminate the middleman. The Planters Company moved to Virginia from Wilkes-Barre a few years later.

MR. PEANUT
Reg. U. S.
Pat. Off.

There's a word for good Peanuts ...and Peanut Candy

Planters 5¢ Peanuts

Planters PEANUT CANDY JUMBO BLOCK 5¢

YES, only the world's peanut experts can roast and salt peanuts the way PLANTERS do. And only PLANTERS can make those big Jumbo Blocks taste so good.

You'll love those big, Virginia peanuts, roasted and salted to crisp perfection. In the cellophane bag, they're famous as America's Nickel Lunch. More energy than in meat, fish or eggs.

And PLANTERS famous Jumbo Block is pure peanut candy at its very best. They're both only 5c each —both Planterrific!

These PLANTERS products are also made in Toronto, and sold everywhere in Canada.

PLANTERS is the word for PEANUTS

In 1916, "Mr. Peanut" was introduced to the public. The Planters Company conducted a sketching contest among high school students in Suffolk to aid in their search for a trademark that would symbolize its major product, the peanut. The winning sketch was of an anthropomorphized peanut, and a commercial artist then added a top hat, cane, and monocle. The Mr. Peanut logo became, and still is, one of the most widely recognized of trademarks. It is found on all kinds of novelty items: buttons, knives, glasses, trays, that were made in profusion in the 1930s and 1940s. There even is an organization for collectors of Mr. Peanut items: Peanut Pals, The Associated Collectors of Planters Peanuts Memorabilia.

Planters retail stores began appearing on the scene in the 1930s on a large scale. Perhaps the most famous of the Planters stores was at 1560 Broadway in New York City. It was called The Peanut Store and displayed the processing of peanuts from planting to the retail store product. A monstrous illuminated sign, above the storefront, contained 15,000 light bulbs and an animated Mr. Peanut, twenty feet tall, pointing to a circle in which different Planters products flashed on and off. The words *Planters Peanuts* flashed on and off, too, in neon, and peanuts "flowed" from a bag at the bottom of the sign.

One of the items featured in the circle was the Planters Peanut Bar. Made of peanuts, sugar, corn syrup, and salt, this bar became a big hit almost the instant it came on the market.

Planters was acquired by Standard Brands in 1961, and in 1981 became a part of Nabisco Brands, Inc. The Planters Peanut Bar, consequently, will continue to keep the Mr. Peanut trademark in the public eye.

Long Live the Turtle

I f handed a piece of chocolate pecan caramel candy people will almost always say, "Why, that's a Turtle!" The Mr. Turtle symbol, used to identify Turtles, is a trademark that's widely recognized and deserves a place alongside Mr. Peanut as one of the two top candyland symbols. DeMet's, Inc., began operating in 1898. The best product to emerge from the DeMet's candy kitchens, Tur-

tles, were first sold from DeMet's retail stores as loose candy pieces. In 1966, Turtles were also sold in package form (two to a pack), in aluminum-foil bags. That line was discontinued in 1975, when a wrapper for the Turtles bar was introduced. The Turtles bar is now sold through other retail outlets as well as in vending machines. (Turtles also come boxed.) Two other bar products now being produced by DeMet's, Inc., are Buttermallow and French Mint, which first appeared in the marketplace in 1978.

You'll Get a Chuckle out of This One

Fred W. Amend started in the candy business in 1875, when, at the age of sixteen, he went to work in the plant of the Henry Heide Company in New York City. At the time, Heide's specialty was almond paste, and candy was only a sideline. So began a string of jobs for Amend in the candy business. In 1887, he started working for Dr. Beeman's Pepsin Gum. By 1900, he was selling mainly bulk candy for Whitman's in the Chicago area. One of the products he sold for Whitman became a rather well-known boxed candy called the Whitman Sampler. In 1915, Amend and his son, Fred B. Amend, became employees of the Paul F. Beich Company, operating Beich's Chicago plant.

In March of 1921, Fred W. Amend went into business for himself, manufacturing marshmallow. Later that year, he began producing jelly candy from a formula he himself had developed. The formula solved what was then the single largest problem confronting makers of jelly candy — the outbreak of "sweat" on the surface of the jelly pieces. Fred's wife suggested the trade name Chuckles for the new product, which hit the market in 1921. The jellies were wrapped by hand in a rolled package. A twist at each end of the roll kept the candies from falling out. Today, Chuckles are packaged to compete with candy bars sold on store counters.

The Amend factory occupied one floor of a loft building in an area of Chicago known as the Kingsbury District. One of the other floors in the building Amend rented was leased by the Walter H. Johnson Company, makers of the PowerHouse bar. But there were many candy companies in the district, among them E. J. Brach, Bunte, F. W. Rueckheim & Bro. (Cracker Jack), Shotwell, and Pan Confection.

Much of the early Amend output was bulk candy, sold mainly to syndicate stores; F. W. Woolworth was the largest customer. With business growing, a new location was needed. In the Chicago factory one of Fred Amend's greatest sources of annoyance was the freight elevators in which raw materials came up to be made into candy and the finished products went down to an underground tunnel system then being used in the Chicago Loop area. So Amend built a one-story factory in Danville, Illinois, in 1930. One of the bonuses of the Danville location was that shipments going to the East did not have to pass through Chicago.

At the start of World War II, Chuckles became the center of an extensive advertising campaign started by the Amend Company. The campaign was launched in twenty-one large markets east of the Mississippi River and north of the Mason-Dixon Line. Billboards, car cards, newspapers, and radio stations were used to promote the product. Two of the slogans for promoting "Chuckles — 5 flavors — 5¢, America's favorite jelly candy" were "Purest candy,

tastes just dandy, keep it handy" and "Best candy buy in town."

During the last years of the war, 65 percent of the company's production was under government contract for rations, special PX packages, and other military requirements. At the end of the war, Chuckles was the only product manufactured.

In 1949, Spice Drops came along; in 1965, jelly-centered candies with a hard sugar coating. In 1968, another type of jelly candy, known generically as jujubes, was added to the line. This candy had less moisture in the center than other jelly items, and its surface was oiled. In 1970 the Fred W. Amend Company was sold to Nabisco Confections, Inc.

In September of 1974, Chuckles teamed up with Evel Knievel, a motorcycle daredevil. Knievel wore Chuckles patches on his skysuit, his crash helmet, and his rocket-powered Sky-cycle. His attempt to jump the Snake River Canyon in Idaho turned into an ambitious promotional campaign. With national coverage, Knievel's stunt brought much free publicity to Chuckles, but it wasn't too successful for Knievel.

The Sky-cycle was to be launched off a 108-foot ramp at "a speed exceeding a moon shot." At takeoff, a little over halfway up the ramp, parachutes opened prematurely. Knievel and the Sky-cycle didn't make it across the canyon; they parachuted into the canyon, crashing into rocks at the river's edge. Helicopters and boats joined in the rescue attempt and brought Knievel to safety.

The Chuckles products of today, such as the original Chuckles, Chuckles Cinnamon Softees, and Chuckles Cherry Jellies, come in different kinds of packaging and are nationally distributed. Today, just as it was over fifty years ago, Chuckles remains in the front rank as "America's favorite jelly candy."

There's a Sucker Born Every Minute

Like P. T. Barnum, Bobby Riggs was a showman who believed Americans wanted to be fooled. Riggs, known as "the Happy Hustler," was a very good amateur tennis player who became a top professional player. In 1956, Riggs dabbled around with exhibition tours of tennis matches, and even tried launching a series of barnstorming baseball tours between two teams of American and National League All-Stars. Thirteen games were played before the project folded because of poor crowds.

Riggs somewhat disappeared from the public eye until the early 1970s, when he came up with the idea of offering a challenge to women tennis players. His defeat of Margaret Court Smith (known as "the Mother's Day Massacre") set the stage for September 20, 1973, when what was billed as "the Tennis Match of the Century" and "the Battle of the Sexes" was to come off at the Houston Astrodome.

Riggs, then fifty-five years old, had as an opponent the much younger Billie Jean King, a champion at tennis and a real fighter for women's rights. Riggs played the promotional aspects of the match to the hilt. Of King, Riggs said, "She's a great player for a gal. But no woman can beat a male player who knows what he's doing. I'm not only interested in glory for my sex, but I also want to set women's lib back twenty years, to get women back into the home, where they belong."

The Houston Astrodome was packed with a live audience (32,000), and forty-three million watched the match on TV. The audience saw King blast Riggs off the court, 6–4, 6–3, 6–3.

What the live audience and millions on TV also saw was the result of one of the more ambitious advertising blitzes for a candy product, a caramel sucker known as Sugar Daddy. Riggs did all kinds of promotional stunts to bring the sucker to the attention of the public, and he was ideally suited to the image of a sugar daddy.

The Houston Astrodome performance had a real circus air to it. Bobby Riggs, wearing a Sugar Daddy jacket and holding on to a giant-size Sugar Daddy, arrived at courtside in a rickshaw drawn by a team of young ladies called "Bobby's Bosom Buddies."

Riggs presented the giant Sugar Daddy, weighing twenty-two pounds and made especially for the occasion, to King before the live crowd and the huge TV audience. It was estimated that the show generated prime-time coverage that was worth about $90,000 a minute — or, at thirty minutes, $2,400,000 worth of national coverage. Sugar Daddy as a product wasn't mentioned by the announcers, but the visual exposure was there. Sugar Daddy, a good seller in the past, got a real sales boost during that promotion campaign.

The story of Sugar Daddy as a confectionery product starts with Robert Welch, who sold chocolate-coated fudge in 1922 on the streets of Cambridge, Massachusetts. Welch sold the fudge at three pieces for ten cents and did a land-office business as a candy hawker until he went into the candy-making business for himself. He devised his own brand of chocolate-covered fudge and called it Avalon. The name dates back to the Arthurian legends; the Island of Avalon was where King Arthur was carried after he was mortally wounded in battle.

112

Robert Welch's brother, James, joined him in the business for a while early on. Then, in the summer of 1925, Robert decided to venture out on his own. He went into the caramel business, using 22 percent cream to make a really rich caramel product. Sticks were inserted into the caramel slabs so that they could be handled easily. The form capitalized on the current popularity of lollipops. Various slogans were tried out for the new product; the one selected was "Of All the Pop Family, This Is the Papa." Thus the genesis of the Papa sucker name.

In 1926, national distribution was planned for the bar, and Robert Welch went to open a manufacturing plant in the center of the candy industry, Chicago. He took the Papa sucker along with him, and brother James remained in Cambridge to start a new business for himself.

Lack of business closed the Chicago plant in 1928, and Robert opened a new operation in Brooklyn, New York, in 1929. Here, Papa suckers were produced for about three years. While operating that factory, Welch also went to work for the E. J. Brach Company of Chicago, spending three years with that confectionery outfit. He commuted by air between New York and Chicago on alternate weeks.

The Papa sucker was produced at both the Brooklyn plant and the Brach plant in Chicago, and in 1931 or 1932 the name was switched from Papa to Sugar Daddy. The term "sugar daddy" was a popular one at the time and is better than "papa" in suggesting a wealth of sweetness.

In 1932, Robert Welch left Brach's and also closed his Brooklyn plant. Since Brach's was, at that time, no longer interested in producing candy bar items, Welch took Sugar Daddy along with him. He opened a confectionery operation in Attica, Indiana, for a few years before rejoining his brother back in Cambridge.

James Welch, by now, had the James O. Welch Company operating in fine fashion. When his brother came back in 1935, James took over production, and Robert handled sales and advertising. (Robert remained until 1956, when he left to form the John Birch Society.)

James O. Welch's first candy factory was a one-room plant in a building in Cambridge. The year was 1927. Another occupant of that building, located on the second floor, was a fellow who tried to interest the other tenants in a new idea he had for plastic film. That fellow, Edwin H. Land, named the film Polaroid.

Welch produced a single product to begin with in that one-room plant. It was a chocolate-covered fudge bar that became known as Welch's Fudge. Some other bar products that made their appearance were Welch's Frappe Bar (a chocolate-covered nougat) and Welch's Cocoanut, which came along in 1931 and was a national popular seller by the 1940s. Welch's Brazil Nut Fudge and Welch's Pecan Penuche were two early uncoated bars; Chocolate Stars and Chocolate Covered Raisins were other products.

When Robert joined James and brought Sugar Daddy with him, the product became one of the real confectionery fixtures of the company. Given the success of the Daddy, Sugar Mama made its appearance in 1935, but was around for only a few years before retiring. The Sugar Mama was reintroduced in a slightly different form in 1965 as a chocolate-covered caramel sucker, and is still marketed today.

One of the more effective sales campaigns conducted by Robert Welch for Sugar Daddy was carried out in 1941–1942. An agreement was signed with a comic features syndicate to produce Comic Cards (similar to baseball cards). Various prizes were offered to those who sent in the Comic Cards, but avid collectors often ignored the prizes, preferring to build up their card collections and swap duplicates with friends.

Adults, as well as kids, saved the cards packed with Sugar Daddy suckers. King Farouk of Egypt was especially fond of the Comic Cards, and wrote to Robert Welch in hope of completing his collection.

Robert Welch was responsible for numerous slogans used to sell Sugar Daddy in his years with the company. One of the more popular ones appeared in the late 1940s: "Oh, What a Sucker!" Today, Sugar Daddy comes in several sizes, but no matter what the size, it's still "the longest lick on a stick."

A 1948 introduction of the James O. Welch Company, Pom Poms, milk chocolate–covered caramel balls, were an immediate success. The name derived from the word *pom-pon*, an ornamental ball or tuft used on clothing, caps, and fancy costumes. On the boxes of Pom Poms, ladies in fancy, hooped dresses promenaded across the front panel.

The James O. Welch Company became part of Nabisco Confections, Inc., in 1963, and today is known not only as a leader in producing candy items, but also as an innovator in advertising, promotion, and merchandising.

Mickey and Ann and Itty Bitty Candy

Burlesque returned to Broadway with a bang in the late 1970s, when *Sugar Babies* opened on Broadway. The ageless Mickey Rooney (alias Andy Hardy) and the incomparable Ann Miller teamed with a host of other talented people to bring a rollicking production to the stage.

Included in the cast was a bevy of beauteous females called the Sugar Babies. One of the numbers the bevy sang and danced to was "Let Me Be Your Sugar Baby."

In the popular vernacular of burlesque days "sugar babies" were the young women on whom middle-aged "sugar daddies" spent bundles. Sugar Babies, soft, caramel tidbits, were first introduced to the market in 1935. They were launched because of the success of Sugar Daddy, the caramel sucker.

During the stage performance of *Sugar Babies*, one of the things the audience looked forward to was having handfuls of Sugar Babies tossed out from the stage. The official stage program carried in the credits the following notice:

Sugar Babies® manufactured by Nabisco Confections, Inc. All proceeds from sale of Sugar Babies Candy will be donated to charity courtesy of Nabisco Confections.

The James O. Welch Company was the originator of Sugar Babies, now being produced by Nabisco Confections, Inc.

A Tasty Debut

When James O. Welch sat in on the Broadway stage performance of *Junior Miss*, he liked the play very much, and he also liked the name Junior Miss. First appearing as stories in *The New Yorker* by Sally Benson concerning the trials and tribulations of Judy Graves, a teen-ager, the series was made into a 1941 stage play that ran on Broadway for 710 performances. Patricia Pearson starred in the role of Judy Graves. In 1942, "Junior Miss" premiered on radio, starring Shirley Temple. With a progression of stars in the role of Judy Graves, the show remained on radio into the early fifties.

The name of the play stuck in the mind of James Welch, and several years later he parlayed Junior Miss into a candy product. When he did, he came up with the name Junior Mints, for miniature, chocolate-covered mint patties.

Advertising copy written for salesmen in 1949 read:

Many a junior miss will beam happily as she sparkles her way into the social limelight, and all the interested young men make her the toast of the town. But we still expect all of you interested young men, and even those not so young, to make our JUNIOR MINTS the most successful debutante of the fall season. For if you'll excuse the expression we use, Junior Mints has got what it takes.

Salesmen took Junior Mints to heart and did make the product a success on the market. The year was 1949, and Junior Mints has been going strong ever since.

Straight from Switzer-land

A delicious aroma arises when you open a letter from the Switzer Candy Company. The yellow stationery has black printing on it, and that ink is impregnated with the scent of licorice, which certainly tingles the olfactory nerves.

Located in St. Louis, Missouri, Switzer has a number of advertising slogans. One of their best is "The world's best licorice comes from Switzer-land."

In 1884, Frederick M. Switzer and Joseph B. Murphy founded the Murphy & Switzer Candy Company. Murphy was a candy maker; Switzer, an entrepreneur. The company's name was changed in 1888 to the F. M. Switzer Company, and in 1890 to the Switzer Yellow Jacket Company. That name was derived from a molasses kiss candy manufactured by the company.

By 1916, the Switzer Licorice Company was established. Cherry and chocolate "licorice" were added to the black licorice line in 1920. A strawberry "licorice" was added in 1977. The different-flavored "licorices" were eventually packaged in wrappers as "bars" for placement in candy bar sections of stores. Switzer merged with Beatrice Foods Company in 1966, and became the Switzer Candy Company in 1972. In 1981, the Good & Plenty Manufacturing Company became part of the Switzer operation. Founded approximately eighty years ago, the Good & Plenty line includes such items as its well-known licorice candy, Good & Plenty, and its fruit candy counterpart, Good 'n Fruity. This means that not only great licorice will continue to flow from Switzer-land, but other candy of merit as well.

Starting a Business on Peanuts

In April of 1925, the Tom Huston Peanut Company was born in Columbus, Georgia. The sole product was Tom's Toasted Peanuts, which quickly became a good seller in the South. Other new products were introduced in following years, among them Tom's Peanut Bar, which was on the market in the late 1920s.

Though Tom's products established a solid selling base in the South, it wasn't until World War II that they became recognized on a national basis. At the PXs in many Army camps in the South and Southwest, G.I.s from other sections of the country first met the line of Tom's products. A favorite snack treat of airmen at Texas Air Force bases was a packet of Tom's Peanut Butter Sandwiches (peanut-butter sandwiches between cheese crackers), which went along splendidly with a bottle of 3.2 beer.

In 1962, the McAfee Candy Company, Inc., in Macon, Georgia, was purchased by Tom's. A line of coconut, chocolate, and hard candies was added to a general line of over 300 snack products now being manufactured by Tom's, all sold nationally. The official name of the company became Tom's Foods in 1970, and the firm now is a wholly owned subsidiary of General Mills, Inc.

Some of the candy bars being produced by Tom's are Park Avenue, My Buddy (a chocolate-flavor-covered nut roll), and the Full Dinner bar. Some other bar products are Tom's Toasted Peanut Roll, Tom's Peanut Butter Log, Tom's Fudge, Peanut Butter Pals, and Peanut Butter Crunch.

The Columbus plant has a series of peanut storage silos that are 143 feet high — equal to the height of a fourteen-story building, and covering an area nearly the length of a football field. At the end of September each year there are about twenty-seven million pounds of peanuts in storage in those silos. "That ain't peanuts!"

Salvatore, Salvatore, and Anello

Salvatore Ferrara came to the United States from Italy in 1900. He worked as a dishwasher, a railroad foreman, and as an interpreter for other Italians for eight years before he'd saved enough money to open a pastry shop in Chicago. Among his products were the multicolored sugar-coated almonds that Italians call *confetti*. His confectionery products became so popular, he decided to set up a separate company to make them.

Around 1919, Salvatore Ferrara formed a partnership with his brothers-in-law, Salvatore Buffardi and Anello Pagano, and the business grew and grew. A new factory eventually was built in Forest Park, Illinois, where the Ferrara Pan Candy Company is now being run by the second and third generations of the founders.

All Ferrara Pan Candy Company products, which come in colorful boxes, are popular items at the candy counters in stores and theaters. Some of the old-line products are Jaw Breakers, Boston Baked Beans, Red Hots, and Atomic Fire Balls. More recent products are Alexander the Grape, Lemonhead, Fruit Cocktail Imperials, Cherry Chan, and Jelly Beans Candy.

The word "Pan" in the company's name refers to two candy-making processes, the hot pan process and the cold pan process. The hot pan process gives us hard-shelled candies, like Jaw Breakers. In this process, each tiny grain of sugar actually becomes a piece of candy. In a heated

copper pan, hot liquid sugar is poured over granules of sugar while the pan rotates. The hot liquid sugar adheres to each sugar grain, and the grain gradually increases in size, crystallizing into a hard ball of candy. When each of the hard balls of candy reaches a desired size, flavor and color are added, and the candy pieces are polished to make them look attractive.

Unheated stainless steel pans are used in the cold pan process, which starts with a center, such as a peanut in Boston Baked Beans or a hard candy center, as in Lemonheads. A mixture of corn syrup, sugar, and gum arabic causes the granulated sugar to adhere to the center piece. As in the hot pan process, ingredients, color, and flavor are added until the pieces reach the desired size.

Regardless of what pan process is used, Ferrara Pan Candy Company products certainly have panned out well over the years.

Deep in the Heart of Texas

In 1938, a confectionery company was born in Lufkin, Texas. Atkinson Candy made use of the Lone Star of Texas and ran its name, Atkinson's, across the middle of a star, thus forming the logo on each kind of candy bar the company produced.

Four candy products emerged from the Atkinson Candy Company. The Peco Brittle bar has a regular brittle base with peanuts and chip coconut added. The Rainbow Coconut bar is a semifirm bar made of sugar, corn syrup, and coconut, and is a colorful bar, with two pink strips of eating goodness on either side of a center white strip. Mint Stick and Chick-O-Stick were two other 1938 items.

Chick-O-Stick is a honeycombed candy filled with peanut butter and rolled in toasted coconut. When originally introduced in 1938, it was called Chicken Bone. The name was changed to Chick-O-Stick in 1955, when interstate shipments began.

A 1947 item, Peanut Butter Bar, contains a peanut-butter honeycombed center with a hard candy jacket. It joins the products mentioned above as one of the stars of the regionally distributed Atkinson line.

Cheer, Cheer for Old Notre Dame

Claeys Candy, of South Bend, Indiana, was started in 1919 by Jerome C. Claeys. The first candy bar produced, the Eatabar, was a caramel nut bar with a maple-flavored icing. The firm's best-selling bar during the 1930s and through the sixties was Puff Ball. Both Eatabar and Puff Ball were discontinued when manufacturing costs rose too rapidly.

In the 1970s and up to the present, Claeys Creme Fudge has met with excellent consumer acceptance. The Claeys Creme Fudge bars come in various flavors: Real Chocolate, Vanilla, Peanut Butter, and Coconut.

While not in the candy bar category, some other Claeys products are of nostalgia value. Claeys produces a line of old-fashioned sugared hard candies in seven flavors, which are packed in wooden kegs used by dealers for display. The flavors? Sassafras, wild cherry, spearmint, lemon drops, anise, and horehound.

All candy lovers know there's something in South Bend to cheer about besides Notre Dame.

Charlie and the Chocolate Factory

Roald Dahl's famous character, Willy Wonka, first made his appearance in the book *Charlie and the Chocolate Factory*. The rights to use the name Willy Wonka on confectionery products belong to the Willy Wonka Brands Division of Sunmark, Inc.

Skrunch, a milk chocolate, peanut-butter, and peanut bar, and Oompas, double-flavored (chocolate and peanut) pieces of sugar-coated candy, were originally launched by the Quaker Oats Company in 1970. Those products, along with the Willy Wonka name for candy products, were purchased by Sunmark in 1972 through its Concorde Confections Division. And in 1980, Concorde Confections and Breaker Confections, another Sunmark company, merged to form the Willy Wonka Division.

The Breaker Confections Division first manufactured Tart N Tinys, small dextrose tablets that are both sweet and sour, in 1969. Then came Wacky Wafers, fruit-flavored wafers, in 1971. Bottle Caps, a soda pop–flavored candy tablet, hit the market in 1973, and Everlasting Gobstoppers, jawbreakers that change colors and flavors, was a 1976 entry. The name Gobstoppers, by the way, comes from Dahl's book.

Some other Willy Wonka brands are Daredevils, which are "devilishly hot" jawbreaker candies, Volcano Rocks, Candy Sneaks, Just Juice, Dinasour Eggs, and Mix Ups.

SKRUNCH.
BUTTERIER AND SKRUNCHIER
NET WT.
OZ.(40.7g)

Best Wishes
Willy Wonka

just juice
The great taste of fruit

BOTTLE CAPS.

WACKY WAFERS
deliciously different candy artificially

SLIDE TOP OPENER
tart·n tinys
CANDY

SLIDE TOP OPENER
VOLCANO ROCKS. candy

flip
'n take
DISPENSER

EVERLASTING
GOBSTOPPER.
JAWBREAKER MIDGETS
NET WT.
1.6 OZ.(45.3g)

oz. (45.3 g)

Baby Scale

When Samuel Born gave birth to a new confection in Brooklyn in the 1920s, he decided to dramatize the event by placing a baby scale next to the candy in the window of his shop. On a placard by the scale were the words "Just Born Candies," and from that incident the corporate identity of Just Born, Inc., grew. The corporate symbol now includes a baby in a scale.

A popular pair of names in use during the twenties was Mike and Ike, and Samuel Born decided that combination would make a good name for his fruit-flavored candies. Boxes of Mike and Ike first appeared in the marketplace in 1928. Making their appearance the same year were Hot Tamales, boxed cinnamon-flavored candies.

In 1932, the company moved from Brooklyn to Bethlehem, Pennsylvania, its present location. Jolly Joes (grape-flavored candies) were introduced in 1960, and Cool Kids (spearmint candies) arrived in 1962. Another Just Born product, manufactured under the Maillard Corporation brand, got into the news when President Ronald Reagan took office in 1981. The product, Teenee Beanees, is a gourmet line of jelly beans.

Chattanooga Choo Choo

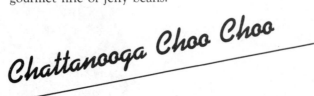

Glenn Miller immortalized Chattanooga, Tennessee, with his Big Band rendition of the hit pop tune of 1941, "Chattanooga Choo Choo." In the confectionery line, Chattanooga is also known for the Brock Candy Company.

William Emerson Brock was a North Carolina country boy whose family moved to Winston-Salem when the farming life didn't pan out. After a few years as clerk in a general store, Brock was hired as the first road salesman to work for the Reynolds Tobacco Company. Mr. Reynolds, president of the company, told a friend he was looking for the greenest, "countriest" boy he could find to put on the road to sell tobacco. W. E. Brock was hired, quickly became a master salesman, and within a few years was division sales manager, with headquarters in Chattanooga.

Brock saved his money, and by 1906 got out of the tobacco business by buying a small candy company. He renamed the company the Brock Candy Company. Now, W. E. Brock didn't know anything about candy, but he did know sales. The confectionery products at that time were principally penny candies and bulk, packed in wooden pails, and none was individually wrapped or packaged.

Mr. Brock's first manufacturing venture was coconut bonbons. At the time, the Henry Heide Company of New York was considered to have the best coconut bonbon on the market. Brock's new product was priced two or three cents a pound higher than Heide's, but when salesmen complained, Brock replied that the only way to prove that his was better was to charge more for it. The ploy worked, and Brock Cocoanut Bon Bons quickly became excellent sellers.

In the early 1920s, a five-cent Peanut Butter Stick was developed. It became the biggest sales item on the roster of Brock Candy products.

During World War II, a nut roll called the Brock Bar was manufactured. It contained peanuts and was low in sugar content, ideal characteristics, in light of both the sugar rationing brought on by the war and the popularity of nut rolls in the South. The bar was very popular, but was discontinued in the sixties, when production costs skyrocketed.

A dark chocolate–covered Fudge Bar was also produced at this time, as was the Marshmallow Bar, which consisted of honey and corn syrup, whipped up as marshmallow, with a corn-flake covering.

It was during this same period that the Brock Candy Company began sponsoring a radio program. One of the more popular jingles of the time originated on that radio program. The jingle went: "Stop Where You Are, Buy a Brock Candy Bar." The jingle really helped to boost sales of Brock Bars as well as other bar products.

The Brock Company now concentrates on a general line of packaged candies, since it no longer makes bars. A subsidiary, however, Schuler Chocolate, Inc., of Winona, Minnesota, does manufacture a bar, Cherry Humps. Distributed by L. S. Heath and Sons Company of Robinson, Illinois, the Cherry Humps bar was particularly popular in the 1940s. Schuler also made another popular forties' item,

Duck Lunch, a bar that contained toasted corn flakes. Duck Lunch paired with the Chicken Dinner bar from the Sperry Candy Company made for an interesting counter display.

Here's a tip of the hat to a real entrepreneur, W. E. Brock. He made it all the way to the top with just a third-grade education. The company that bears his name is living proof that he was a salesman of the first order.

BROCK is a dandy buy
A nickel is all you pay,
B-R-O-C-K
Buy a BROCK today!

Where the Corn Grows Tall

In 1878, Sioux City, Iowa, was a frontier town. That year, Edward C. Palmer started his food company and in the early 1900s began manufacturing confectionery products.

In the thirties, candy bars became an important part of the sales of the Palmer Candy Company. By the mid 1950s, over thirty different candy bars had been experimented with, though only the four best-selling bars were kept in production.

The Bing bar (1931) has a cherry cream center enveloped in a chocolatey coating thick with chopped peanuts. The Twin Bing bar (1950s) contains two Bings in one wrapper. The La Fama bar (1919) has an Italian cream center, pecans, and a milk chocolate coating. The Peanut Cluster bar (early 1900s) has a vanilla cream center and is coated with milk chocolate chock full of roasted peanuts.

Until 1977, the Palmer Candy Company sold only regionally in ten Midwestern states. Today the frontier has expanded, and Palmer bars are distributed in forty-seven of the forty-eight continental states.

Chew Awhile

Kids went wild when, in 1962, the Phoenix Candy Company came out with the Now & Later bar. Each Now & Later bar consists of several individually wrapped taffy squares, and the bars are available in close to fourteen flavors. The name Now & Later was selected to suggest to customers that they eat some of the taffy squares in the bar right away and save the rest for another occasion.

The Phoenix Company goes back to 1919, when a little candy company in Brooklyn, New York, was turning out penny saltwater taffy. In 1953, the company became the Phoenix Candy Company, which struck gold with its product Now & Later.

Phoenix, now a division of Beatrice Foods Company, devotes most of its production operations to turning out Now & Later in order to keep all those taffy-chewing kids out there happy.

An Earthquake Couldn't Shake It

The 1906 earthquake that devastated much of San Francisco did little damage to an area of the city known as Jackson Square. Located there was the first large chocolate manufactory of Domingo Ghirardelli. Born in Italy, where he learned the confectionery and chocolate trade, Ghirardelli immigrated to the United States via Uruguay and Peru in 1849, lured to the Golden West by incredible tales about the rush for gold. He engaged in several business ventures before building his first large factory.

The business became quite successful, and larger quarters were eventually needed. So a square block of property, part of the former Jackson Square, on North Point Street, overlooking San Francisco Bay, was purchased. It became known as Ghirardelli Square. No longer a chocolate factory, Ghirardelli Square now houses a series of shops and restaurants and is one of the better-known tourist attractions of San Francisco.

Ghirardelli died in 1894, but various kinds of chocolate candy bars, as well as Ghirardelli's Ground Chocolate, are still being turned out at the present location of the Ghirardelli Chocolate Company, in San Leandro, California. Ghirardelli chocolate bar products bear such names as Milk Chocolate with Raisins, Milk Chocolate with Almonds, Milk Chocolate, Milk Chocolate Crisp, Flicks Crisp, Milk Chocolate Munchy Malt, Mint Chocolate, and Dark Chocolate.

Washington, D.C., Head City of the U.S. of A.

President Ronald Reagan has a hankering for a certain kind of candy, and that hankering resulted in national publicity for a confectionery product manufactured by Herman Goelitz, Inc., with headquarters in Oakland, California. The candy is, of course, the jelly bean.

Back in 1878, Gustav Goelitz was selling handmade candy from a horse cart in Belleville, Illinois. Another Goelitz, Herman by name, became the founder of the company bearing his name, by opening a factory in Chicago. Herman Rowland, a fifth generation Goelitz, now oversees the destiny of the company from its head location in Oakland as well as from the old Chicago factory location. Jelly beans are the main product.

When President Reagan was governor of California, he regularly ingested the jelly beans turned out by Goelitz. A portion of a letter from the former governor said, "We can hardly start a meeting or make a decision without passing around a jar of jelly beans. Thanks for helping state government run smoothly."

It was almost twelve years before he would taste the new gourmet jelly bean that burst on the scene in 1976.

The Jelly Belly, the official name of the original gourmet jelly bean, currently comes in thirty-six flavors. Natural flavors are blended into the heart of the bean to produce such varieties as blueberry, guava, jalapeño, and tangerine. About eighteen million Jelly Belly jelly beans roll off the production line each day, approximately 480 to a pound.

Seven thousand pounds of Jelly Belly beans arrived in Washington for the Reagan-Bush inauguration. That was approximately 3,360,000 little beans, enough not only for all the Republicans present, but also for some of the Democrats, who found they were tasty too.

Where the Deer and the Antelope Play

Bill and Dorothy Harmsen decided to move to the foothills of the mountains in Colorado and buy ten acres of ranchland, complete with a big barn and a just barely modern farmhouse. The big barn became a candy factory, and Jolly Rancher Candies was the result.

The first Jolly Rancher candy bar product was a five-cent hot cinnamon taffy stick now known as Fire Stix. Since that bar was introduced in 1951, numerous other flavors have been added to the Stix line. Today, regular bar flavors are, in addition to Fire Stix, Watermelon Stix, Apple Stix, Strawberry Stix, Grape Stix, and Cherry Stix. Many other flavors are also available in smaller bars.

Jolly Rancher, in Wheatridge, Colorado, carries on a national radio advertising campaign, and is now a division of Beatrice Foods. The company owns its own fleet of trucks, and ships to all fifty states. The trucks carry a flavor of the West to cowhands all over who prefer reaching for a candy bar rather than a six-shooter.

Little Orphan Annie

Ovaltine Products, Inc., was long established before it capitalized on the name Ovaltine in the making of a candy bar. The year was 1981 when the Ovaltine Crunch Bar, milk chocolate and barley malt among other things, made its appearance on candy counters.

Back in the 1930s, Ovaltine was the long-time sponsor of one of the most popular radio programs of all time for kids. Millions of children tuned in faithfully each day to listen to the adventures of Little Orphan Annie. The program was the genesis of the adventure serial on radio.

Each show opened with the announcer, Pierre André, introducing the theme song. The lyrics varied over the years; perhaps the most popular was:

Who's that little chatterbox?
The one with pretty auburn locks?
Who can it be?
It's Little Orphan Annie.
She and Sandy make a pair.
They never seem to have a care.
Cute little she,
It's Little Orphan Annie.
Bright eyes
Cheeks a rosy glow
There's a store of healthiness handy.
Pint-size
Always on the go
If you want to know
"Arf," goes Sandy.
Always wears a sunny smile.
Now wouldn't it be worth your while,
If you could be,
Like Little Orphan Annie?

To make certain you didn't forget who the sponsor was, Annie would comment, "Leapin' Lizards, Ovaltine is good!" And Pierre André would tell you about the current Annie premium that was being offered. Two of the most popular premiums were the Ovaltine shake-up mug (complete with pictures of both Annie and Sandy), and a decoder necessary for deciphering the daily clues given at the end of each broadcast. (The clues were never earthshakers, but that didn't bother an avid Annie fan, because what counted was the anticipation — even after countless disappointments — that the clue might really turn out to be a wowzer!)

The radio Annie was based on the comic strip by Harold Gray. The story is told that Gray's original strip had a boy, not a girl, as the main character, but a quick sex change was performed on the strip sample, giving birth to the redhead, Little Orphan Annie. The first published strip appeared on August 5, 1924. The first radio broadcast was on April 6, 1931. By 1940, the radio "Little Orphan Annie" had run its course, so Ovaltine dropped sponsorship and took up with "Captain Midnight," who also became one of the great premium-givers of the air.

Seldom were two programs so successful in imprinting a product name on several generations of people as were "Captain Midnight" and "Little Orphan Annie." If you're old enough to be in one of those generations, you'll have pleasant memories of childhood every time you see an Ovaltine Crunch Bar on a candy counter.

Caramelville

Go a little north of Fort Wayne, Indiana, and you'll bump into Kendallville. That's the home of one of the factories that make Kraft Caramels, so the town has been nicknamed "Caramelville" by its residents. Garland, Texas, is where another Kraft plant is located, so it could be called the Caramelville of the Southwest.

James Lewis Kraft started out as a wholesaler of cheese in Chicago in 1903. His initial total assets of $65 went to renting a horse named Paddy and a wagon, and buying a small stock of cheese that he sold to grocers in the city. J.L. prospered, and after a few years in the cheese-making business, he was on the road to gaining world renown for Kraft products.

During the Depression, J.L. looked around for a product besides cheese that contained milk and that his salesmen could carry with them on their routes. What was more natural, then, than getting into the caramel business? Kraft found the confectioner in the Chicago area who was the most knowledgeable in caramel production and put him to work. By 1933, a nickel caramel bar was produced, but grocers weren't too keen on stocking caramels year round. Caramels were considered primarily summer replacements for chocolate.

Kraft caramel pieces were also manufactured that year, and they eventually caught on quite successfully in the marketplace. One of the popular packets on the market today, individually wrapped caramel pieces enclosed in a cover wrapper, is sold in the candy bar sections of many stores.

In 1934, just a year after Kraft Caramels were introduced, the makers of Kraft dairy products began sponsoring a radio variety show that became one of the outstanding musical shows on radio, "Kraft Music Hall." Running for just over a decade, the program starred such performers as Al Jolson, Paul Whiteman, and Bing Crosby.

Putting Town Hall to Good Use

During the Depression, Katharine Beecher made butter mints in her home in Manchester, Pennsylvania. She made them for relatives and friends, and by chance some of those mints found their way to a hotel in nearby Harrisburg. The mints were served as after dinner mints to guests in the hotel dining room and were found to be quite tasty. One guest thought them so tasty that he looked up Mrs. Beecher and made her an offer.

Katharine Beecher agreed to the offer, and a hot-selling product was in the works. So many orders poured in that neighbors had to be hired to keep up with production. When space became a problem, Mrs. Beecher rented the Manchester Town Hall for her candy business. Without a doubt, the sweetest business ever conducted in a town hall was carried out during that occupation!

In 1949, a new factory was constructed, and in 1974, Katharine Beecher Candies was taken over by the Pennsylvania Dutch Company, but it still operates as a separate division. In addition to Beecher Candies, the Charlie the Candyman line and many varieties of Wilbur Chocolate Bars are also distributed.

The Pennsylvania Dutch Company in Mt. Holly Springs, Pennsylvania, markets some 500 candy and specialty food items nationally. Included in the confectionery line are several candy bars. The Pennsylvania Dutch Peanut Butter Bar has a milk chocolate covering, and the

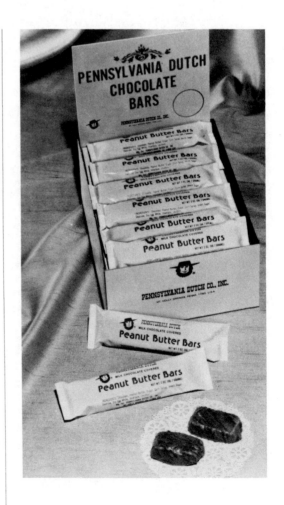

Pennsylvania Dutch Peanut Chew Bar has a dark chocolate covering.

A registered trademark of the Pennsylvania Dutch Company is Hector Hinkle, whose face appears on the bar products. Hector has a full beard, wears a hat, and has a big smile on his face. He's probably smiling because he's either had, or is about to have, one of the many good Pennsylvania Dutch confectionery products.

Just Remember Pearl Harbor

The Boldemann Chocolate Company began manufacturing chocolate and cocoa in San Francisco in 1885. The company's main business was, and still is, chocolate coating and cocoa products. Many years later, in part to create a market for its own chocolate coating, it introduced a line of candy bars.

Many Boldemann bars were popular sellers in the 1930s, among them Boldemann's Toffee Chocolate, Boldemann's Milk Chocolate, Boldemann's Milk Chocolate with Almonds, and Boldemann's Malto Milk Chocolate. Some other bars were Boldemann Vitamin B$_1$ Bar, and Boldemann Aristo Milk Chocolate Wafers Bar.

The line of chocolate bars was manufactured until shortly after the attack on Pearl Harbor. The controls and quotas set by the War Production Board during World War II led the Boldemann management to feel that raw materials could be put to better advantage by manufacturing only coatings and bulk products. So Boldemann stopped making candy bars.

The Boldemann Chocolate Company, now a division of Blommer Chocolate Company of Chicago, is still alive and kicking in Union City, California, producing its well-known chocolate coating. Such retail items as Milk Chocolate Pokies and Peanut Pokies are also made and sold nationally.

Open Sesame

Whenever Ali Baba in *The Arabian Nights' Entertainments* wanted to open the door of the robbers' den, he spoke the magic words "Open sesame!" The command was a form of tribute to the sesame plant, an important Middle East crop whose flat seeds yield an edible oil.

One of the earliest candies recorded contained sesame seeds; it was made by the Turks as far back as 3000 B.C. The candy was called halvah, and consisted chiefly of ground-up sesame seeds, to which honey was added.

Today, commercial halvahs are often made with such additives as artificial preservatives, hardeners, egg albumen, and refined sugars. Fantastic Foods, Inc., of Novato, California, however, produces halvah in bars closely following the ancient recipe. The bars are produced in three flavors, Natural Halvah Sesame Honey, Natural Halvah Carob-Sesame, and Natural Halvah Cashew Currant. Labeled snack bars rather than candy bars, they are available nationally through health food stores.

Let the Sun Shine In

LIK-M-AID was the first major success of what is today known as Sunline Brands. Sunline began, in 1931, as the Fruzola Company, operating in Salt Lake City, Utah. Although it manufactured various confectionery items, Fruzola's main business was soft-drink products.

In 1952, it became apparent that LIK-M-AID would have national appeal, and the company moved its facilities to St. Louis and established the name Sunline.

LIK-M-AID, "the candy that pours," was initially packaged in one-cent and five-cent packets. It was a powdered candy that could be eaten from the pack, sprinkled on other foods, made into a drink, or used in a variety of other ways. The product was a pioneer in the "sour candy" field. One spin-off confectionery item was SweeTARTS. SweeTARTS, compressed candy tablets, first appeared in 1963. Available in small packets, this item, along with other Sunline products like the Tangy Taffy bars, is found in candy bar sections of retail stores.

Not a Berra or a Bear but a Bar

Yogi Berra? No. Yogi Bear? No. Yogi Bar? Yes. Begun in 1979 as a kitchen production for family and friends, within two and a half years the bar had become the major product of a new manufacturer, the Good Life Company, which was selling its product internationally. The company manufactures and distributes the natural-food Yogi Bar, the ingredients of which are honey, dates, raisins, peanuts, figs, almonds, cashews, chick pea flour, crisped rice, whole wheat flour, and safflower oil. Good Life Company also makes Yogi Carob Bar, Yogi Hawaiian Bar, Nut Krackel Sweet, and Spice of Life.

The Good Life philosophy:

> Here's our family of Money Makers
> Standing tall, waiting for takers.
> They're pure and free from nasty things
> That Mother Nature never brings.

Swinging on a Bar

Emil J. Brach was another of the many German immigrants who established themselves in the confectionery business in the United States. Emil became an employee with Bunte Brothers & Spoehr in Chicago in 1881 and in time saved enough money to go into the caramel business for himself. In 1904, he leased a small store in Chicago, retail candy sales in front, and caramel manufacturing in the rear. Two sons joined him, and the business, now known as E. J. Brach & Sons, quickly outgrew several manufacturing locations in Chicago. A large, new facility was built in 1921, and that plant, with numerous additions over the years, is still the company's location.

A line of candy bars was manufactured regularly until 1937, when the company went mainly into the manufacture of bulk, bag, and box goods. Some of the bars featured in a 1920s Brach's catalogue were Brach's Milk Chocolate with Roasted Almonds, Brach's Sweet Milk Chocolate, Brach's Chocolate Peanut Bar, Brach's Cream Cocoanut Bar, Brach's Cream Pecan Bar, Brach's Chocolate Marshmallow Bar, Chocolate Cherry Bar, Chocolate Pineapple Bar, and Brach's Black Walnut Fudge.

Three of the early Brach bars had distinctive names. There were the "Huck" Finn Peanut Bar and the Zolo-Nut Bar (maple-flavored base, marshmallow, Spanish peanuts, and a chocolate covering). The Polo Bar had the same contents as the Zolo-Nut Bar but was more egg-shaped. For some unknown reason the name Polo was discontinued and was replaced by the name Owl.

After 1937, E. J. Brach & Sons produced only a few kinds of bars on a sporadic basis. During World War II, for example, the armed forces were supplied with such items as Mint Bars, Almond Nougat Bars, Coconut, and perhaps the company's best-remembered bar product, Brach's SWING Bar. Brach's SWING Bar was one of the top-selling candy bars of the late 1940s. The bar, a chocolate-covered peanut-butter honeycombed item, had a wrapper that carried the legend "Ask for BROX" to help with pronunciation of the Brach name.

Perhaps the most intriguing Brach bar names were three that had numbers in them. The three bars were simply called Broxie No. 1, Broxie No. 2, and Broxie No. 3.

Brach's still makes plenty of candy, but it no longer makes bars. Because of the bars it has produced, however, the company name has an honored place in Candy Bar History. Time was when much of America prefaced its order for a candy bar by saying, "Make it a BROX bar."

141

Candy Industry, May 23, 1950

Hooray for Hollywood

The Hollywood Candy Company got its start not in Hollywood, California, not in Hollywood, Florida, and not even in Hollywood, Minnesota, but in Minneapolis, Minnesota, in 1912. Early on, the Hollywood star symbol appeared as a part of the design of each wrapper. In 1936, the company made a move to Centralia, Illinois, where it is still located.

One of the early Hollywood confectionery products capitalized on the affection the public had for the milk shake: the Double Milk Shake candy bar. The Double Milk Shake was a combination of chocolate-flavored nougat, caramel, and milk chocolate covering. Some time after 1934, Double was dropped from the name and the bar simply became the Milk Shake bar.

Another early bar had a white chocolate coating; it was originally known as the Double Zero bar. The Double Zero also dropped the first part of its name some time after 1934, and simply became the Zero bar. Pay Day, a salted peanut–covered fudge center bar, appeared in 1932. It quickly became a best seller for the Hollywood Company.

An early bar that is no longer around was the Three Little Pigs. The bar probably received its name from the popular Walt Disney cartoon of 1933 that captured the hearts of the public.

NET WT. 2 OZ

Hollywood's Butter-Nut
5¢ 5¢
Milk Chocolate
NUTS AND CARAMEL
MFD. BY HOLLYWOOD CANDY CO., CENTRALIA, ILL.

"Butter-Nut"

Hollywood
BUTTER NUT
CARAMEL AND PEANUTS
NET WT 1.5 OZ 42 g
BUTTER NUT

Some other Hollywood Candy bars were Polar (1924), Butter-Nut (1916), Hollywood Milk Chocolate (1922), and Assorted Nut Fudge. A 1936 introduction, Red Sails, was a good seller in the 1950s, as was a bar called Smooth Sailin. Also popular in the fifties was the Hail bar. The Big Time bar made its appearance in 1940. And the 3 Bears Bar was selling in the fifties. Of these bars, only Butter-Nut, now Butter Nut, is still around.

A bar named after an airplane appeared in the seventies. The 747 bar featured a drawing of the 747 aircraft on the wrapper.

A disastrous factory fire in 1980 caused a temporary halt to candy bar production. But a new factory now in operation in Centralia assures the buying public that all its Hollywood favorites from Illinois — Milk Shake, Zero, and Pay Day — will still be around.

144

Nuts to You

Perley G. Gerrish worked as a journeyman carpenter for several years before investing in a business of his own. He acquired an interest in the Squirrel Brand Company in 1899 (it had been started nine years earlier). The company specialized in packaging and selling fancy nuts to the carriage trade.

Gerrish began changing the image of the company almost immediately. He wanted to make Squirrel Brand nut products available to the general buying public, so he introduced the first five-cent Squirrel Brand bag of peanuts in 1900 and began expanding the company nut line to include candy products.

After working on his original formula for a peanut bar, Gerrish introduced the first peanut bar to an eager buying public in 1905. The first Squirrel Brand Peanut Bar was a penny item. It became available in a five-cent size in later years. A five-cent chocolate-coated peanut bar was sold in the years 1932 through 1937.

A candy item containing nuts, Squirrel Brand Nut Caramels, has been a favorite of both kids and adults for many years. First sold in a one-cent size, it was later made in a two-cent size. Squirrel Brand Chews are also now available in a five-cent bar size and come in seven versions: grape, red cherry, mint, banana, watermelon, and two old-time favorites, Nut Caramel and Nut Zippers. No matter which one you choose, you'll get a good chewy mouthful.

And Then There Were More

The following is a list of candy bar manufacturers that did not find their way into earlier pages of this book. One or more bars produced by each manufacturer are noted except in cases where general confectionery products are the main output of a company. To the best of my knowledge, these bars still exist; those no longer in existence are indicated with an asterisk. Should the author be in error, he would be glad to find out that the announcement of a bar's death is premature.

Company	Bars
American Licorice Co. San Francisco, California	Licorice Whips Red Whips
Amurol Products Co. Naperville, Illinois	Dipsticks
Andes Candies, Inc. Delavan, Wisconsin	Creme de Menthe Ting-A-Ling Petite Solid Milk Chocolate Bar
Annabelle Candy Co., Inc. Hayward, California	Rocky Road Big Hunk Look U-No
André Prost, Inc. Old Saybrook, Connecticut	
Asher Brothers New Hyde Park, New York	
Walter Baker Chocolate and Cocoa Co. Dorchester, Massachusetts (now a division of General Foods Corp.)	Baker's Milk Chocolate* Baker's Milk Chocolate Almond* Baker's Caracas (Sweet Chocolate)* Baker's Milk Chocolate with Malted Milk Crunch*
Barton's Candy Corp. Brooklyn, New York	Mint Cream Bar Peanut Butter Bar Delite
Beacon Sweets, Inc. Newark, New Jersey	

Company	Bars
Bishop Candy Co. Los Angeles, California (became subsidiary of Walter H. Johnson Co. in 1944)	Bishop Fudge* Cherry Flip*
Blommer Chocolate Company Chicago, Illinois	
Bonita Candies Inc. Fond du Lac, Wisconsin	Bonita Leaping Lena Candy Bar*
Brown and Haley Tacoma, Washington	Mountain Bar
Bunte Candies, Inc. Chicago, Illinois (now located Oklahoma City, Oklahoma)	Tangos* Fine Mint Chocolate Creamy Cakes*
Callard & Bowser White Plains, New York	
The Candy House, Inc. Nacogdoches, Texas	
Candymaster, Inc. Minneapolis, Minnesota	Coffee Dan*
Cella's Confections, Inc. New York, New York	Chocolate Covered Cherries
Charms Company Freehold, New Jersey	
Cocoline Chocolate Co., Inc. Brooklyn, New York	
Cook Chocolate Co. Chicago, Illinois	Vita Sert*

Company	Bars	Company	Bars
Dairy Maid Chocolate Co. Newark, New Jersey	Dairy Maid Marshmallow bar* Dairy Maid Milk Chocolate Covered Peanuts* Dairy Maid Nonpareils* Dairy Maid Milk Chocolate Covered Raisins*	Hagler Candy Co. Chicago, Illinois	Opera Cream Bar*
		William Hardie Co. Cleveland, Ohio	Jinks*
		Heidelberger Confectionery Co., Inc. Philadelphia, Pennsylvania	Heidelberger's Jersey Style Cream Rolls* California Style Jellies*
Deran Confectionery Co. Cambridge, Massachusetts	My Baby* Campfire Chocolate Covered Marshmallow Bar Wyler's Thirst Quenchers Borden Peppermint Patty	Hi Energy Food Products Chico, California	
		Walter J. Hirsch Co. Chicago, Illinois	Mazie* Van-Toy*
		Hoopers Confections, Inc. Oakland, California	
Doscher's Candies Cincinnati, Ohio		Hoosier Candy Co. Indianapolis, Indiana	Williamson's Wellmade Almond Butter Toffee*
Duer Sales, Inc. Chicago, Illinois	Carlton Bar* Carlton Nut Roll* Carlton Dip*	John Horne Co. Evanston, Illinois	John Horne's Coconut Waffle* John Horne's Coconut Bon Bon*
Eddyleon Chocolate Co., Inc. Garden City, New York			
Elgin Chocolate Products Co. Elgin, Illinois	Log Jam*	The House of Bauer Chocolates Lincoln, Nebraska	
		Howard Johnson Co. Boston, Massachusetts	
Elmer Candy Corporation Ponchatoula, Louisiana	Gold Brick	Huyler's New York, New York	Metropolitan Sweet Chocolate Cakes*
The Estee Corporation Parsippany, New Jersey	Natural Carob Bars	Idaho Candy Company Boise, Idaho	
Eton Chocolates, Inc. Chicago, Illinois		Inter Mountain Trading Co. Berkeley, California	Bear Valley Concentrated Food Bars
Euclid Candy Co. Chicago, Illinois San Francisco, California	Skipper* Full of Almonds Candy Bar* Dolly Dimples* Love Nest* Big Game* Best Pal*	Jacobson's Des Moines, Iowa	Jacobson's Baby* Jacobson's Dairy Maid Cherry* Jacobson's Dairy Maid Maple*
Fort Worth Candy Co. Fort Worth, Texas	Commando*	W. E. Jacobs Candy Co. Chicago, Illinois	Betsy Ross*
Gilliam Candy Co. Paducah, Kentucky	Cat-Tail* Tummy Full Peanut Bar*	Joyva Corporation Brooklyn, New York	Joyva Halvah Joyva Sesame
Glade Candy Company Salt Lake City, Utah		Judson Candies, Inc. San Antonio, Texas	Chewy Pralines Toppers
Harvey L. Gladstone, Inc. Hummelstown, Pennsylvania		Kayeless Corp. Wyckoff, New Jersey	
		Keppel's Inc. Lancaster, Pennsylvania	Marshmallow Twist Bar Rainbow Coconut Bar

Company	Bars	Company	Bars
Kimbell Candy Co. Chicago, Illinois	Twin Smacks Bar* Stacks Big Mo Coconut Stacks	A. G. Morse Co. Chicago, Illinois	Texas Nip* Winning Lindy* Morse's Walnut Egg* Morse's Fruit and Nut*
Klotz Confection Co. Louisville, Kentucky	Klotz's Nutty Brittle*	Ben Myerson Candy Co. Los Angeles, California	Christopher's Peanut Cluster
Kreem Maid Fudge Co. Bethlehem, Pennsylvania (became a division of Just Born, Inc., in 1949)	Kreem Maid Fudge Blocks*	National Candy Co. St. Louis, Missouri	Hippo Peanut Bar*
Lanzi Candy Co. Chicago, Illinois	Cashew Nut & Rice Crunch Coconut & Rice Crunch	Natural Protein Products, Inc. Hayward, California	Jack La Lanne Hi-Protein Bar Honey-Coconut Bar
Leaf Confectionery, Inc. Chicago, Illinois	Whoppers	Nellson Candies, Inc. Los Angeles, California	Nellie's 100% Natural Candy Bars
Sol S. Leaf Chicago, Illinois	Sir Prize Egg*	Ohio Confection Co. Cleveland, Ohio	O.C. Chocolate Pecan Fudge*
Liberty Orchards Company, Inc. Cashmere, Washington		Old Dominion Peanut Corp. Norfolk, Virginia	Betteryet Peanut Candy Bar
James P. Linette, Inc. Reading, Pennsylvania		Pangburn Company, Inc. Fort Worth, Texas	
Lucy Ellen Candies Sullivan, Illinois	Brown Pudding* Shore Dinner* Holiday* Lucy Ellen Chocolate Almond Bar*	Pez Candy Orange, Connecticut	
		Ragold, Inc. Chicago, Illinois	Velamints
Marshall Field & Company Chicago, Illinois		Richardson-Vicks Wilton, Connecticut	Tigers Milk Nutrition Bars
Marshall & Norman Candy Co. Chicago, Illinois	Ice Man Sandwich*	Robinson Foods Fairfield, Iowa	Paradise
Maxfield Candy Co. Salt Lake City, Utah	Pecan Logs Cashew Logs	E. Rosen Co. Pawtucket, Rhode Island	
McKenzie Co. Cleveland, Ohio	Old Hickory*	Runkel Brothers Co. Chicago, Illinois	Headlights*
Melba Sweets Co., Inc. Cliffside Park, New Jersey	Melba Jelly Beans* Melba Licorice Lozenges* Melba Spearmint Leaves* Black Knights*	Russell Stover Candies Kansas City, Missouri	
		Ryan Candy Co., Ltd. New York, New York	Hopalong*
Melster Candy Co. Cambridge, Wisconsin	Brownie Bar*	Miss Saylor's Chocolates, Inc. Alameda, California	Saylor's Almond Crunch* Saylor's Chocolate Royals* Saylor's Mint Patties*
Merrill Candy Co. Merrill, Wisconsin	Merrillite Cherry Cream Puff* Merrillite Cool Wave* Cool Wave*	Shotwell Manufacturing Co. Chicago, Illinois	"Shur-Mac"* "Hi-Mac"* Big Yank*
Mi-Jeans Candies Waterloo, Iowa	Milk Ceylon*	Sifers Confection Co. Kansas City, Missouri (now owned by Hoffman Candy Co. of Los Angeles)	Sifer's Ozark Ridge Candy Bar* Valomilk Dips*

Company	Bars
Sophie Mae Candy Corp. Atlanta, Georgia (division of Fine Products Co., Inc., Augusta, Georgia)	Salted Peanut Roll
Sperry Candy Co. Milwaukee, Wisconsin	Denver Sandwich* Chicken Dinner* Koko Krunch* Cold Turkey* Cool Breeze* Snow-Maid*
Howard B. Stark Co. Milwaukee, Wisconsin (now in Pewaukee, Wisconsin)	Snirkles Stark Candy Wafer Roll
Straightshooter Candy Co. Kansas City, Kansas	
Stuckey's Eastman, Georgia	Golden Gopher Coco Almond Patty Pecan Puff
Tania's, Inc. Denton, Texas	Tania's Raisin Nut Crunch Apricot Cashew Crunch
Tastysnack, Inc. Windsor, Pennsylvania	
Texarkana Candy Co. Texarkana, Texas	Good Scout Peanut Brittle Candy Bar*
Tree of Life, Inc. St. Augustine, Florida	Natural Carob Candy Bars
Ucanco Candy Co. Davenport, Iowa	Ol' Timer* Knockout*
Van Engers, Inc. Chicago, Illinois	Baby Lobster* License* Van Load* September Morn*
F. B. Washburn Candy Corp. Brockton, Massachusetts	Waleeco Pepp-Stick Bar* Waleeco Peanut Bar* Waleeco Coconut Bar
Whitman's Chocolate Division, Pet Incorporated Philadelphia, Pennsylvania	Capers
C. & J. Willenborg, Inc. Ramsey, New Jersey	
Henry Witty Chicago, Illinois	Opera Roll*
George Ziegler Candy Co. Milwaukee, Wisconsin	Giant Bar*

National Candy Buyers Bar Survey

ach year two of the magazines serving the confectionery industry, *Candy Industry* (formerly *Candy & Snack Industry*) and *Candy Marketer Quarterly*, conduct a survey. Up until 1982 it was called the National Candy Buyers Bar Survey (now the National Candy Buyers Brands Survey). The 1981 survey was the last to be conducted on a regional basis. The regions reflected popular national brands as well as popular regional brands.

In the 1981 survey (also in 1982), Snickers was number one across the country. Various brands jockeyed around from region to region for the second through twentieth positions, with several bars often sharing the same slot. The make-up of the regions were:

- **Northeast:** Maine, New Hampshire, Vermont, Massachusetts, Rhode Island, Connecticut, New York, New Jersey, and Pennsylvania.

- **Southeast:** Delaware, Maryland, District of Columbia, Virginia, West Virginia, North Carolina, South Carolina, Georgia, Florida, Kentucky, Tennessee, Alabama, and Mississippi.

- **North Central:** Ohio, Indiana, Illinois, Michigan, Wisconsin, Minnesota, Iowa, Missouri, North Dakota, South Dakota, Nebraska, and Kansas.

- **South Central:** Arkansas, Louisiana, Oklahoma, and Texas.

- **Mountain and Pacific:** Montana, Idaho, Wyoming, Colorado, New Mexico, Arizona, Washington, Oregon, Utah, Nevada, California, Hawaii, and Alaska.

Northeast Rankings

1. Snickers
2. Reese's Peanut Butter Cup
   Hershey Almond
3. 3 Musketeers
   Milky Way
4. Hershey Milk Chocolate
   M&M Plain Chocolate
   Kit Kat
   M&M Peanut Chocolate
5. Almond Joy
   Twix
6. Mounds
   Whatchamacallit
   Nestlé Crunch
7. York Peppermint Pattie
   Rolo
   Mr. Goodbar
8. Summit
   Baby Ruth
   Tootsie Roll
   Clark
   5th Avenue
9. Mars Bar
   Reese's Pieces
   Heath Bar
   Chunky
10. Mallo Cup
    Junior Mints
    Starburst
    Twizzlers
11. Peanut Chew
    $100,000 Bar
12. Krackel
    SweeTARTS
    Star Bar
    Zagnut
    Go Ahead
13. Oh Henry!
    Jumbo Block
    Whoppers
    Cella's Cherries
    Raisinets
    Andes Creme de Menthe
    Goetze's Caramel Creams
14. Chuckles
    Butterfinger
    Chew-ets
15. Bit-O-Honey
    Charleston Chew!
16. Nature Valley Granola
      Bars
    Cadbury Milk Chocolate
    Oompas
17. Munch
    Jujyfruit
    Milk Duds
    Mason Mint Patty
    Mason Crows
18. Super Scrunch
    Switzer's Licorice
    Tootsie Pops
    Smoothie
    Mellomint
19. Rothchild's
    Pay Day
    Hot Tamales
    Mike & Ike
20. Good & Plenty
    Quaker Oats Granola Bars
    Mason Dots
    Mentos

Southeast Rankings

1. Snickers
2. Reese's Peanut Butter Cup
3. 3 Musketeers
   M&M Plain Chocolate
   M&M Peanut Chocolate
4. Milky Way
   Hershey Almond
5. Baby Ruth
   Hershey Milk Chocolate
   Kit Kat
6. Whatchamacallit
   Almond Joy
   Mars Bar
   Butterfinger
7. Nestlé Crunch
   Mounds
   5th Avenue
   Twix
   Mr. Goodbar
8. Pay Day
   Clark
   Reese's Pieces
   Zero
9. Summit
   Zagnut
   York Peppermint Pattie
   Heath
   Peanut Chew
10. Rolo
    Raisinets
    Chunky
    SweeTARTS
11. Goobers
    $100,000 Bar
    Tootsie Roll
    Milk Duds
12. Twizzlers
    Junior Mints
    Crispy
    Starburst
    Goo Goo Cluster
13. Star Bar
    Sugar Babies
    Hershey Big Block
14. Caramello
    Hot Tamales
    Whoppers
    Mellomint
15. PowerHouse
    Super Scrunch
    Goetze's Caramel Creams
    Boston Baked Beans
16. Bit-O-Honey
    Jujyfruit
    Jordan Almonds

17. Butter Nut
    Oh Henry!
    Sno-Caps
    Dum Dum Pops
18. Claeys Fudge
    Jawbreakers
    Red Hots
19. Tootsie Pop Drops
    Mallo Cup
    Charleston Chew!
20. Chuckles
    Skittles
    Reese's Crunchy Peanut
       Butter Cup

North Central Rankings

1. Snickers
2. 3 Musketeers
    M&M Plain Chocolate
3. M&M Peanut Chocolate
    Hershey Milk Chocolate
    Hershey Almond
4. Reese's Peanut Butter Cup
    Milky Way
5. Baby Ruth
    Whatchamacallit
    Butterfinger
6. Kit Kat
    Mars Bar
7. Twix
    Heath Bar
    Nestlé Crunch
8. Almond Joy
    Salted Nut Roll
    Mr. Goodbar
9. Summit
    Clark
    Pay Day
10. Mounds
    Chunky
    $100,000 Bar
    Junior Mints

11. Whoppers
    Rolo
    Twin Bing
    Zagnut
    Skittles
12. York Peppermint Pattie
    Milk Duds
    Tootsie Roll
    Munch
13. Sno-Caps
    Now & Later
    Raisinets
    Go Ahead
    Goobers
    Jolly Rancher Stix
14. Marathon
    Charms Pops
    Jujyfruit
    Charleston Chew!
    Reese's Pieces
15. Chuckles
    Goetze's Caramel Creams
    Oh Henry!
    Krackel
16. Sixlets
    Choco'Lite
    Mentos
    Sugar Babies
    PowerHouse
17. Wayne Bun
    Mason Dots
    Nature Valley Granola
       Bars
    5th Avenue
18. Crispy
    Turtles
    Nestlé Milk Chocolate
19. Goo Goo Cluster
    Pom Poms
20. Claeys Fudge
    Oompas

South Central Rankings

1. Snickers
2. M&M Peanut Chocolate
3. M&M Plain Chocolate
    3 Musketeers
    Reese's Peanut Butter Cup
4. Hershey Almond
    Hershey Milk Chocolate
5. Milky Way
    Butterfinger
    Baby Ruth
6. Kit Kat
    Almond Joy
    Mars Bar
7. Nestlé Crunch
    Mr. Goodbar
    Pay Day
8. Twix
    $100,000 Bar
    York Peppermint Pattie
    Whatchamacallit
9. Krackel
    Mounds
    Heath Bar
10. Rolo
    SweeTARTS
    Summit
    Junior Mints
    Go Ahead
11. Raisinets
    Mounds
    Salted Nut Roll
    Super Scrunch
12. Chunky
    Reese's Crunchy Peanut
       Butter Cup
    Milk Duds
    Almond Joy
13. PowerHouse
    Clark

14. Bit-O-Honey
    Zagnut
    Whoppers
    Munch
15. Tootsie Roll
    Oh Henry!
16. Jumbo Block
    Nature Valley Granola
        Bars
    Tootsie Pop Drops
17. 5th Avenue
    NECCO Wafers
18. Skittles
    Sugar Babies
19. Caramello
    Nestlé Milk Chocolate
20. Cherry Mash
    Smoothie

Mountain and Pacific Rankings

1. Snickers
2. 3 Musketeers
   M&M Peanut Chocolate
   M&M Plain Chocolate
3. Milky Way
   Twix
4. Hershey Almond
   Reese's Peanut Butter Cup
5. Kit Kat
   Mars Bar
   Hershey Milk Chocolate
6. Butterfinger
   Baby Ruth
   Almond Joy
7. Starburst
   Summit
   Chunky
   Whatchamacallit
   Rolo

8. Nestlé Crunch
   Tootsie Roll
   Pay Day
   Salted Nut Roll
   Skittles
9. $100,000 Bar
   Junior Mints
   Rocky Road
   Mr. Goodbar
10. Krackel
    Mounds
    York Peppermint Pattie
    Heath Bar
11. Star Bar
    Crispy
    Charleston Chew!
    Milk Duds
    Clark
12. Look
    Oh Henry!
    Marathon
    Bit-O-Honey
13. PowerHouse
    Twizzlers
    Reese's Pieces
14. SweeTARTS
    Switzer's Licorice
    Whoppers
15. 5th Avenue
    Nature Valley Granola
        Bars
16. Caravelle
    Munch
    NECCO Wafers
17. Turtles
    Red Whips
18. Now & Later
    Big Hunk
19. Butter Nut
    Abba-Zaba
20. Nibs
    Flicks

LOG JAM 5¢

Chocolate
VAN-TOY 5¢
CRISP AND CRUNCHY
"Easy to Eat"
WALTER J. HIRSCH COMPANY
CHICAGO, U.S.A.

TRADE MARK REG. U.S. PAT. OFFICE
ALL HEALTHFUL—NUTRITIOUS—PLEASING
ONLY THE VERY BEST AND PUREST INGREDIENTS USED
2 OZ.
©1927

Morse's WINNING
5¢ LINDY

BE SURPRISED!
SirPrize
1¢
5¢ to Egg to 1¢
5¢
NET WEIGHT 1—"
SOL. S. [...]

Morse's
MAPLE
WALNUT
NET WEIGHT 1½ OZ. OR OVER
A. G. MORSE COMPANY
CHICAGO

2 for 5¢
LICENSE
2 for 5¢
WEIGHT 1¼ OZ

The
Betsy Ross
LOVED BY THE NATION BAR
Milk Chocolate Coating

ICE MAN

Net Weight 2½ oz. or over.
Old Fashioned Cocoanut
VANILLA
VANILLA
5¢ JINKS
VANILLA
Old Fashioned Cocoanut
THE Wm. M. HARDIE CO.
Cleveland, Ohio

Author's List of Twenty All-Time Favorites

The list includes bars of the present, plus those that have already taken a trip down Memory Lane. The bars are listed alphabetically.

Bit-O-Honey
Charleston Chew!
Chicken Dinner
Denver Sandwich
Goo Goo Cluster
Heath Bar
Hershey Milk Chocolate with Almonds
Mars Bar
Milk Duds
Nestlé Milk Chocolate
Oh Henry!
Pearson's Salted Nut Roll
PowerHouse
Reed's Butter Scotch
Rocky Road
Snickers
Snirkles
Sugar Daddy
Turtles
Zero

Afterword

Books generally don't have an afterword, but this one does. It closes with the battle cry of all true candy bar lovers:

Go forth and eat!

Photo Credits

Credits are listed by page number. Photos not credited are by the author or from his collection of wrappers and old advertisements. Many candy bar names are registered trademarks. I have credited trademarks only when specifically requested to do so by the company.

Page
3 Texas Nip and Baby Lobster: Courtesy of Glenn Sontag
10 Courtesy of Glenn Sontag, photo by Jack Sevick, Jr.
16–19 Courtesy of Hershey Foods Corporation
21 Goo Goo Cluster and photo of Archie Campbell: Courtesy of Standard Candy Company
23 Standard Brands
26 Coconut Grove and Cocoanut Grove: Courtesy of Glenn Sontag
27 Baseball card: Design courtesy of Topps Chewing Gum, Inc.
28 Courtesy of Paul F. Beich Company
31 Charleston Chew! (right): Courtesy of Nate Sloane
32 Courtesy of Nate Sloane
33 Courtesy of L. S. Heath & Sons, Inc.
34 Heath wrapper and advertisement: Courtesy of L. S. Heath & Sons, Inc.; Heath Milk Chocolate with Peanuts: Manufactured by L. S. Heath & Sons, Inc., Robinson, Illinois
37 Courtesy of Peter Paul Cadbury, Inc.
40–41 Courtesy of Peter Paul Cadbury, Inc.
45 Clark Valuable Wrapper and Crispy wrapper: Courtesy of the D. L. Clark Company; Yellow Gold: Courtesy of Glenn Sontag
46 Advertisement at left: Courtesy of the D. L. Clark Company
47 Courtesy of the D. L. Clark Company
48–49 Courtesy of the D. L. Clark Company
50 Milk Duds: Courtesy of the D. L. Clark Company
51 Tootsie Roll: Courtesy of Tootsie Roll Industries, Inc.
54 Courtesy of M & M/Mars
55 Copyright © Mars, Inc.
57 Courtesy of M & M/Mars
58–61 Wrappers: Copyright © Mars, Inc.
62 Seven Up: Courtesy of Farley Candy Company
65 $100,000s: Courtesy of the Nestlé Company, Inc.
66 Courtesy of Goetze's Candy Co., Inc.
67 Courtesy of Goldenberg Candy Co.
68–69 Heide boxes: Courtesy of Henry Heide, Inc.
70–71 Courtesy of Squibb Corporation
73 Courtesy of Squibb Corporation
74 Courtesy of Charles N. Miller Company
76 Necco wrappers: Courtesy of New England Confectionery Company
78–79 Courtesy of F & F Laboratories, Inc.
80 Courtesy of General Mills
81–84 Courtesy of Cracker Jack Division of Borden Foods, Borden, Inc.
86 Courtesy of the Chocolate House, Inc.
88–90 Courtesy of Spangler Candy Company
95 Copyright Boyer Bros., Inc.
96 Courtesy of Wilbur Chocolate Company
97 Courtesy of Glenn Sontag
98 Bit-O-Coconut: Courtesy of Hollis Gerrish
99 Courtesy of Glenn Sontag
101 Courtesy of the Terson Company

Page
102 Display boxes: Courtesy of the Terson Company
104–105 planters and mr. peanut are trademarks owned and used by Standard Brands, Incorporated, a wholly-owned subsidiary of Nabisco Brands, Inc.
106–107 Courtesy of DeMet's, Inc.
109 Photo of Evel Knievel: Courtesy of Nabisco Confections, Inc.
112 Sugar Daddy: Courtesy of Nabisco Confections, Inc.; photo of Bobby Riggs and Billie Jean King by Curt Gunther; photo of Bobby Riggs by Ken Reagan
115 Welch's products: Courtesy of Nabisco Confections, Inc.
116 Photo of Ann Miller and Mickey Rooney by Martha Swope
117 Courtesy of Nabisco Confections, Inc.
119 Courtesy of Switzer Candy Co.
120 Courtesy of Tom's Foods, Ltd.
123 Courtesy of Atkinson Candy Company
125 Courtesy of Willy Wonka Brands
126 Courtesy of Just Born, Inc.
128 Courtesy of Brock Candy Company
129 Courtesy of Palmer Candy Company
130 Now & Later: Courtesy of Phoenix Candy Company; Ghirardelli's Sweet Vanilla Chocolate Bar: Courtesy of Ben Myerson; Ghirardelli's Chocolate: Courtesy of Ghirardelli's Chocolate Company
131 Courtesy of Herman Goelitz, Inc.
132 Copyright Jolly Rancher Candies, Wheat Ridge, Colorado
133 Ovaltine® is a registered trademark of Ovaltine Products, Inc., Villa Park, IL
135 Courtesy of Pennsylvania Dutch Co., Inc.
136 Courtesy of Ben Myerson
137 Courtesy of Boldemann Chocolate Co., Inc.
139 Courtesy of the Good Life Company
140 Broxie wrappers: Courtesy of Glenn Sontag
141 Courtesy of E. J. Brach & Sons, Divison of American Home Products Corporation
144 747: Courtesy of Jerry Soltis
145–146 Courtesy of Squirrel Brand Company
151 Hopalong: Courtesy of Hollis Gerrish
152 Capers: Courtesy of Pet Incorporated; Dipsticks: © trademark property of Amurol Products Co.
157 Texas Nip, Baby Lobster, Fruit and Nut, Mazie, Opera Roll: Courtesy of Glenn Sontag; photo of buttons: Hake's Americana & Collectibles
158 Courtesy of Glenn Sontag

Color Section

1 Advertisements for Baby Ruth and Welch's Fudge: Reprinted by permission of Nabisco Brands, Inc.
2 Ping: Copyright Mars, Inc.
3 Bitter-Sweet: Courtesy of Hershey Foods Corporation
4 Toffifay: © August Storck KG; Ding a Lings: Courtesy of F & F Laboratories, Inc.; Whoppers: Copyright Leaf Confectionery, Inc.
5 delite: Barton's Candy Corporation; Park Avenue: Courtesy of Tom's Foods, Ltd.; Chick-O-Stick: Courtesy of Atkinson Candy Company
7 Advertisement for Chuckles: Reprinted by permission of Nabisco Brands, Inc.